SIOUX
warriors of the plains

CHIEF SPOTTED-ELK.
SIOUX.

SIOUX
warriors of the plains

Michael Johnson

CHARTWELL
BOOKS, INC.

This edition published in 2008 by

CHARTWELL BOOKS, INC.
A Division of
BOOK SALES, INC.
114 Northfield Avenue
Edison, New Jersey 08837

ISBN-13: 978-0-7858-2397-1
ISBN-10: 0-7858-2397-2

© Copyright 2008 Compendium Publishing Ltd,
43 Frith Street, London W1D 4SA, United Kingdom.

Cataloging-in-Publication data is available from the
Library of Congress.

Printed and bound in China.

Acknowledgements
Design: Compendium Design/Danny Gillespie
Maps: Mark Franklin

**PAGE 1: Shield by E. A. Burbank (1858–1949), who painted
over a thousand Native Americans.** *This image—and all others
unless specifically credited otherwise—is from the author's
collection*

**PAGE 2: Sioux Chief Spotted Elk, 1899, by E.A. Burbank. Friend
of Red Cloud at Pine Ridge, this was not the Spotted Elk who
became chief of the Minneconjou (subdivision of the Teton
Sioux) who is better known as Big Foot.**

**RIGHT: Brulé war-party—one of Edward S. Curtis's classic
photographs from** *The North American Indian Volume III The
Teton Sioux. The Yanktonai. The Assiniboin.;* **Seattle, 1908.**
*Library of Congress, Prints & Photographs Division LC-USZ62-
46958*

Contents

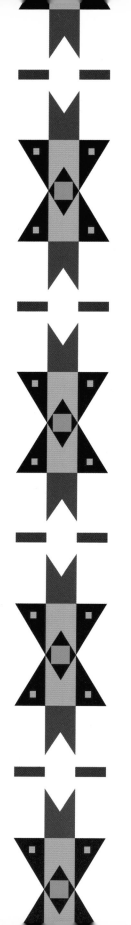

Introduction

Perhaps no tribe of North American Indians is as familiar to the general public as the Sioux. They are famous because of their stubborn resistance to the encroachments of white settlers and battles with the American military. Names of Sioux leaders such as Red Cloud, Sitting Bull, and Crazy Horse have also penetrated the popular consciousness to such an extent that they are virtually household words. Their western branch, the Teton division, was also the most powerful and numerous of the so-called Plains Indian peoples. They had developed a nomadic lifestyle largely dependent upon the shifting herds of buffalo (American Bison) after the rearrangement of the tribal peoples on the eastern and northeastern perimeter of the Great Plains following the Colonial Wars of the northeast during the 17th and 18th centuries, and the effects of the fur trade. Such tribes as the Blackfoot, the vanguard of the tribal movement in the north, were already obtaining horses from the Plateau Indians and becoming skilful equestrian warriors and hunters. Other groups were to remain partly sedentary and horticultural occupying the Missouri River valley or continued to be marginally Woodland Indians.

Horses had been introduced to the Southwestern Indians by the Spanish in the early 17th century and they had spread north via intertribal trade ultimately forming vast herds of hardy wild ponies. By the early 18th century the Blackfoot were obtaining horses from the Plateau peoples and by 1780 the Western Sioux were in possession of herds obtained at first in intertribal trading or warfare, or perhaps from direct southern sources. This new cultural phenomenon based upon the mobility through the acquisition of the horse allowed the bison to become a major food supply supplemented by deer and pronghorn and wild foods gathered by women. These recent newcomers to the short grass high plains country also developed the portable bison-skin tipi which—when erected over a framework of lodge-poles—became another essential and distinctive element of Plains material culture and nomadic life.

The Sioux however share a language, culture, and history that not only belongs to the high plains but also to their older prairie and woodland traditions. By the early 19th century three divisions came to be recognized, reflecting geographical, linguistic, and cultural distinctions: Santee (Eastern); Yankton—Yanktonai (Middle), and Teton (Western).

The term Sioux derives from an Ottawa or Ojibwa designation "na-towe-ssi," which was adapted into French as Nadouessioux and subsequently shortened to simply "Sioux." The usual translation is given as "Little Snakes" or "enemies" as an almost continual state of conflict existed between the Ojibwa and Sioux during the fur trade period. As a consequence many Sioux descendants today consider the name "Sioux" as derogatory. However considerable doubt has recently been raised concerning the true original translation which some linguists claim never meant "snakes." The Sioux name for themselves in one of three dialects is Dakota, "allies," which has been

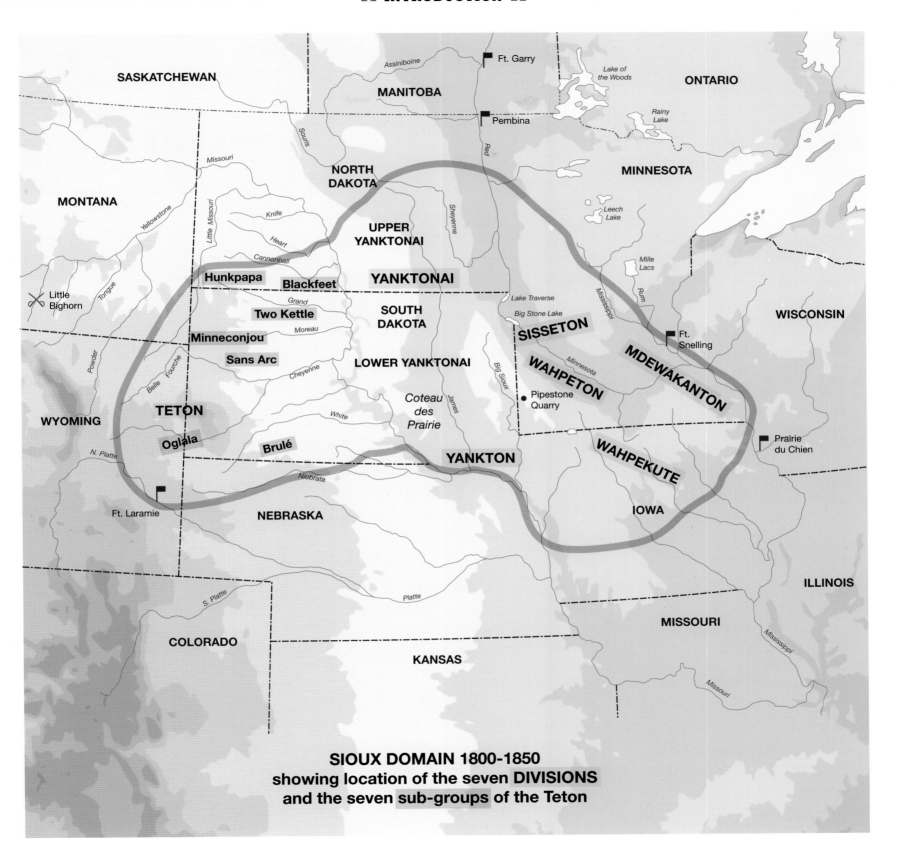

SASKATCHEWAN

MANITOBA

Assiniboine

⚑ Ft. Garry

Lake of the Woods

ONTARIO

⚑ Pembina

Souris

Red

NORTH DAKOTA

Rainy Lake

MINNESOTA

Missouri

MONTANA

Yellowstone

Little Missouri

Knife

UPPER YANKTONAI

Sheyenne

Leech Lake

Heart

Cannonball

YANKTONAI

Mille Lacs

Hunkpapa   **Blackfeet**

Grand

SOUTH DAKOTA

Lake Traverse

Big Stone Lake

Mississippi

Rum

⚔ Little Bighorn

Two Kettle

Moreau

SISSETON

⚑ Ft. Snelling

WISCONSIN

Minneconjou

LOWER YANKTONAI

Minnesota

WAHPETON

MDEWAKANTON

Sans Arc

Cheyenne

Tongue

Powder

Belle Fourche

TETON

White

Coteau des Prairie

Big Sioux

James

● Pipestone Quarry

WYOMING

Oglala

Brulé

YANKTON

WAHPEKUTE

Prairie du Chien ⚑

N. Platte

⚑ Ft. Laramie

Niobrata

NEBRASKA

IOWA

S. Platte

Platte

ILLINOIS

COLORADO

KANSAS

MISSOURI

Mississippi

Missouri

SIOUX DOMAIN 1800-1850
showing location of the seven DIVISIONS
and the seven sub-groups of the Teton

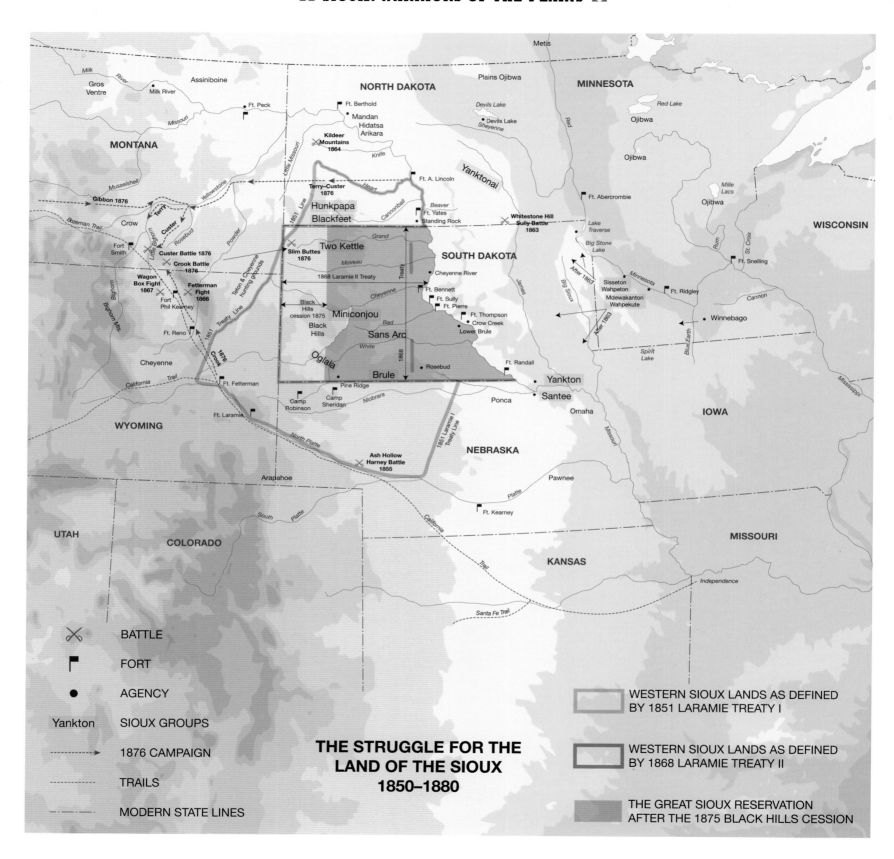

Milk
Gros
Ventre
Assiniboine
River
Milk River
Ft. Peck
MONTANA
Musselshell
Gibbon 1876
Bozeman Trail
Crow
Fort
Smith
Terry
Custer
Little Bighorn
Rosebud
Custer Battle 1876
Crook Battle
1876
Wagon
Box Fight
1867
Fetterman
Fight
1866
Fort
Phil Kearney
Bighorn Mts.
Ft. Reno
Cheyenne
California
Trail
UTAH

NORTH DAKOTA
Ft. Berthold
Mandan
Hidatsa
Arikara
Kildeer
Mountains
1864
Knife
Ft. A. Lincoln
Terry–Custer
1876
Little Missouri
Heart
1851 Line
Hunkpapa
Blackfeet
Cannonball
Beaver
Ft. Yates
Standing Rock
Yellowstone
Powder
Teton & Cheyenne
hunting grounds
Two Kettle
Slim Buttes
1876
Grand
Moveau
1868 Laramie II Treaty
SOUTH DAKOTA
Cheyenne River
Ft. Bennett
Ft. Sully
Ft. Pierre
Cheyenne
Black
Hills
cession 1875
Miniconjou
Bad
Ft. Thompson
Crow Creek
Lower Brule
Treaty
1868
Black
Hills
Sans Arc
White
Oglala
Brule
Ft. Randall
Rosebud
Pine Ridge
Niobrara
Ponca
Camp
Robinson
Camp
Sheridan
Ft. Fetterman
1876
Crook
1851
Treaty Line
North Platte
Ft. Laramie
WYOMING
Arapahoe
South
Platte
California
Platte
Ash Hollow
Harney Battle
1855
1851 Laramie I
Treaty Line
NEBRASKA
Omaha
Ft. Kearney
Platte
Pawnee
COLORADO
Trail
KANSAS
Santa Fe Trail

Metis
Plains Ojibwa
MINNESOTA
Devils Lake
Devils Lake
Sheyenne
Red Lake
Ojibwa
Ojibwa
Ft. Abercrombie
Mille
Lacs
Ojibwa
WISCONSIN
Lake
Traverse
Big Stone
Lake
Whitestone Hill
Sully Battle
1863
Ft. Snelling
After 1863
Big Sioux
Rum
St. Croix
Yanktonai
Sisseton
Wahpeton
Mdewakanton
Wahpekute
Minnesota
Ft. Ridgley
Cannon
After 1863
James
Blue Earth
Winnebago
Spirit
Lake
Mississippi
Yankton
Santee
IOWA
MISSOURI
Independence

BATTLE

BATTLE

FORT

AGENCY

Yankton   SIOUX GROUPS

1876 CAMPAIGN

TRAILS

MODERN STATE LINES

THE STRUGGLE FOR THE
LAND OF THE SIOUX
1850–1880

WESTERN SIOUX LANDS AS DEFINED
BY 1851 LARAMIE TREATY I

WESTERN SIOUX LANDS AS DEFINED
BY 1868 LARAMIE TREATY II

THE GREAT SIOUX RESERVATION
AFTER THE 1875 BLACK HILLS CESSION

widely adopted as an alternative term for the whole tribe, or "Nakota" and "Lakota" in the other two dialects. The earliest European American recordings of the tribe were in 1640; Radisson met some of them in 1660; and Le Sueur traded with them during the 1680s, and reported 27 villages between 1699 and 1702. The Franquelin map of 1697 shows "The Sioux of the East" living almost totally within the present state of Minnesota, around Mille Lacs, and on the eastern tributaries of the Mississippi River. "The Sioux of the West" were first mentioned between 1679 and 1680 living above the falls of Saint Anthony, and a little later they roamed the prairies between the Mississippi and Missouri. These bands were without canoes or horticulture and were outside the area where wild rice was gathered. The French had armed the Ojibwa and were actively engaged in the fur trade, expelling the Sioux from the wild rice areas of Minnesota.

Early European traders also called the Sioux the "Seven Council Fires" as the nation was divided into seven substantial subtribes, four of which form the Santee or Isayati (camp at a knife shaped quarry or lake) and these were:

1. Mdewakanton, "Spirit Lake People" referring to Mille Lacs in Minnesota, sometimes Bdewakanton
2. Wahpekute, "Shooters Among the Leaves"
3. Sisseton, "Ridges of Fish Offal Villagers"
4. Wahpeton, "Dwellers Among the Leaves"

These four subtribes form the Dakota or Eastern division who remained within the present boundaries of Minnesota until 1862. Geographically the Middle Sioux or Nakota division comprised the Yankton-Yanktonai or Wiciyela (those who speak like men):

5. Yankton, "Dwellers at the End Village"
6. Yanktonai, "Dwellers at the Little End Village"

Some doubts have been recently raised as to the true relationship of the Nakota dialect with the Dakota as some scholars believe the difference is not sufficient to warrant separate status.

7. Teton, "Dwellers on the Prairies," the Western Sioux, the largest subtribe outnumbering the other six together, and linguistically the Lakota division.

Interrelationship of the Seven Sioux subtribes with their geographical and linguistic nomenclature

The Sioux language also forms one complete section of the so-called Siouan linguistic language family that had a geographical range which stretched back toward North America's horticultural heartland, the Mississippi, and even to the Ohio country. A number of Siouan tribes were in migration westward during the early historic period. These were the Chiwere group (Oto, Missouri, and Iowa) and the Dhegiha group (Omaha, Ponca, Kansas, Osage, and Quapaw). The Hidatsa and Mandan were already farming the upper Missouri valley centuries ahead of the Sioux historical western expansion. The Crow separated from the Hidatsa to become another true high plains tribe who largely abandoned their farming background. In the eastern United States the Catawba in the Carolinas have been assigned to the same phylum, and a number of minor tribes such as the Saponi, Tutelo, Occaneechi, Ofo, and Biloxi have been tentatively attributed to the Siouan family making it one of the most important on the continent.

Some time during the early historic period the Assiniboine or Stoney Indians are thought to have

LEFT: The struggle for the land of the Sioux, 1850–1880.

Two artist/explorers of the 1830s have left vivid impressions of pristine Native Indian life on the Upper Missouri River. First was George Catlin who between 1830 and 1836 made a number of expeditions to the western plains. During 1833 and 1834 the Swiss artist Carl Bodmer with Prince Maximilian of Wied journeyed along the Upper Missouri painting Indian subjects at trading posts such as Ft. Pierre in Western Sioux country.

LEFT: Chan-Cha-Nia-Tevin Western Sioux woman, wearing a buffalo robe with painted designs. Her dress, which can be seen under the robe, is likely the rare side-fold construction. Painted by Bodmer at Ft. Pierre in June 1833. *All images are from the author's collection unless credited otherwise*

RIGHT: Funeral Scaffold of a Sioux Chief—a print from a painting by Carl Bodmer of a Sioux settlement with a funeral scaffold for a chief. The encampment was near Ft. Pierre. The burial stage in the foreground has a willow cage to protect the remains of a chief from the predations of carrion birds. *Historical Picture Archive /Corbis*

RIGHT: Bear Dance, Sioux by George Catlin. From a sketch made at Ft. Pierre in 1832—one of several versions. "They like the pleasure of a bear hunt and also a participation in the Bear Dance which is given several days in succession . . . all join in a song to the Bear Spirit . . . and must be consulted and conciliated before they can enter upon their excursion with any prospect of success." *Leonard de Selva/Corbis*

separated from the Yanktonai in particular, but more likely from the Dakota in general, moving north to the vicinity of Lake of the Words and Lake Nipigon, Canada. They have viewed and continue to view themselves as branches of the Sioux, using the dialectic term Nakoda to define their language and relationship to their parent tribe. However, their movement to the foothills of the Rockies and Montana plains, their relationships to the Cree and with the Canadian fur trade in reality defines them as an independent tribe.

The author recognizes the popularity of the term "Lakota" today for the Western Sioux, but as this is a linguistic term, has chosen to use the geographical names and the ethnographical terms for the seven subtribes or their divisions and to define people and places in the photographs. This is in accordance with the nomenclature used in *Volume 13, Plains volume of the Handbook of North American Indians*, 2001, Smithsonian Institution, Washington D.C.

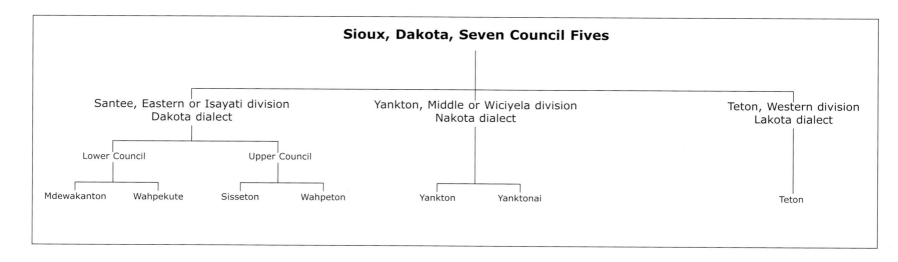

Sioux, Dakota, Seven Council Fives

Santee, Eastern or Isayati division
Dakota dialect

Yankton, Middle or Wiciyela division
Nakota dialect

Teton, Western division
Lakota dialect

Lower Council

Upper Council

Mdewakanton   Wahpekute

Sisseton   Wahpeton

Yankton   Yanktonai

Teton

LEFT: Big Soldier either Western (Teton) or Yankton Sioux painted by Bodmer at Ft. Lookout in May 1833. He wears a shirt decorated with quillwork and hairlock fringes and leggings also with quilled strips and painting. He has a peace medal presented by agents of the United States Government.

Demography

Mdewakanton

One of the seven subtribes of the Sioux Nation, after abandoning the Mille Lacs region in the mid-18th century the Mdewakanton settled on the Rum River and later on the lower Minnesota and Mississippi rivers under pressure from the Ojibwa (Chippewa) Indians. Their principal villages were Kiyuksa, Kapozha (or Kaposia), and Shakopee. After treaties with the United States in 1837 and 1851, they ceded all their lands east of the Mississippi for a reservation along the Minnesota River together with the three other tribes who formed the Eastern or Santee division of the Sioux. After their poor treatment by both government and settlers, which led to the Minnesota uprising of 1862–63, they moved west and north to the Missouri and Canada with few remaining in Minnesota. Their present-day descendents, almost totally merged with other Santee, are enrolled or registered at the Santee Reservation, Nebraska; Flandreau Reservation, South Dakota; on the four small reservations in Minnesota (Upper and Lower Sioux, Shakopee, and Prairie Island); and a few were reported on the Sioux Valley Reserve, near Griswold, Manitoba. In 1823 they were estimated to number about 1,500 in total.

Wahpekute

One of the original Seven Council Fires, and one of the four who constitute the Eastern or Santee division of the tribe, the Wahpekute continued to live in the forested areas of southern Minnesota and Iowa along the Cannon and Blue Earth rivers until the early 19th century. They were closely related to the Mdewakanton and moved with them to the Lower Agency on the Minnesota River in 1851. Today their descendents are at Santee Reservation, Nebraska; Ft. Peck Reservation, Montana; Sioux Valley and Oak Lake, Manitoba; and Wahpeton Reserve, Saskatchewan, but are no longer reported as separate from other Santee. In 1823 they numbered about 800.

Wahpeton

Closely related to the Sissetons, the Wahpeton were one of the Seven Council Fires of the Sioux and one of the four comprising the Santee, or Eastern (Dakota) division of the nation. Their original home was the Minnesota River above Traverse de Sioux but after 1851 they moved northwest toward Big Stone Lake at the northern end of the Sioux Reservation along the Minnesota River. They took part in the uprising of 1862–63 after which they scattered west and north. Their descendents are at Devils Lake (Spirit Lake) Reservation, North Dakota, mixed with Yanktonai and Sisseton; Sisseton (Lake Traverse) Reservation, South Dakota; Flandreau, South Dakota; Bird Tail, Sioux Valley, Sioux Village, Long Plain, and Oak Lake in Manitoba; Standing Buffalo and Wahpeton in Saskatchewan. In 1823 the Long Expedition estimated them to number about 900.

Sisseton

Probably the largest and most important subtribe of Eastern Sioux—and one of the seven forming the nation—the Sisseton was one of the four of the Eastern or Santee (Dakota) division. Before their removal to the northern end of the Minnesota River Sioux Reservation in 1851, their principal location was around the junction of the Cottonwood and Blue Earth rivers with the Minnesota. However their involvement with traders such as the Renvilles had seen some move to Lake Traverse and the James River country. Culturally the Sissetons were very similar to the Yanktonai and formed a link with Sioux groups farther west. They are the main group on the Sisseton Reservation (Lake Traverse) of South Dakota; smaller groups incorporated with other Santees at Devils Lake (Spirit Lake) Reservation, North Dakota; Upper Sioux, Minnesota; Sioux Valley, Manitoba; Moose Woods or White Cap (Cankute Sisseton), Standing Buffalo and Wahpeton (Round Plain), Saskatchewan, Canada. In 1823 they were believed to number about 2,500, probably an underestimate.

Yankton

One of the two subtribes of the Sioux who constituted the Middle or Wiciyela section, although first mentioned in the Leech Lake region of Minnesota in 1683 the Yankton moved southwest into what is now southeastern South Dakota, in the southern Coteau de Prairies along the lower James,

Tree) and the Wasicucica (Half-breed band). In 1823 the Yankton were estimated to number 2,000 and 2,500 in 1868. Their descendents continue to live on the Yankton Reservation and nearby towns in South Dakota.

Yanktonai

The second subtribe of the Wiciyela or Middle branch of the Sioux nation, their historic location was the prairies between the Red River and the Missouri on the upper James and Sheyenne rivers in the characteristically rolling country of the Coteau de Prairies rather than the short-grass country or high plains west of the Missouri. The Yanktonai were divided into two principal divisions: the Upper Yanktonai who comprised about six bands, the Pabaksa (Cut-heads) and Kiyuksa (Breakers of Law) being the most prominent; and the Lower Yanktonai, also known as Hunkpatina (Little Camp at Campo Circle Entrance), who had about nine minor bands. The Upper Yanktonai were finally located on the Standing Rock Reservation, North and South Dakota; Devils Lake (Spirit Lake), North Dakota (Pabaksa band); and a few at Oak Lake, Manitoba. The Lower Yanktonai (Hunkpatina) were settled at Crow Creek Reservation, South Dakota; also Ft. Peck Reservation, Montana mixed with Santees. In 1823 there were 5,200 Yanktonai reported and 4,650 in 1868.

Teton

The Western or Lakota division of the nation was the largest of the seven subtribes, outnumbering the other six together. They were first known to white explorers in the 17th and early 18th centuries—although known as "Sioux of the West" as far back as 1679 when reported on the prairies between the Mississippi and Missouri. With the acquisition of the

Vermillion, and Big Sioux rivers. After hostilities with settlers during the 1850s, the Yankton Reservation was established on the north bank of the Missouri on the Dakota-Nebraska border. The Yankton had a number of bands, probably as many as 13, the most famous being the Cankute (Shooters at the Wood or

FAR LEFT: Eastern (Santee) Sioux brave c. 1864. He is smoking a huge pipe with a "twisted" stem (actually carved) and catlinite head. He also has a gunstock-shaped club and knife sheath. He appears to be sitting on a Hudson's Bay trade blanket.

LEFT: Big Head, Upper Yanktonai Sioux c. 1872. He holds a pipe and eagle feather fan, has fur wrapped braids. Note the beaded blanket strip.

LEFT: Little Wound, Oglala (Teton) Sioux. He wears a magnificent eagle feather trailer warbonnet, beaded shirt, leggings, and moccasins. He holds a pipe and tobacco bag. Photograph Heyn, Omaha, 1899. Photographed probably during Trans-Mississippi Exposition in Omaha in 1898.

RIGHT: Spotted Tail (Sinte Gleska) and wife, Brulé (Teton) Sioux. Richard Hook's oil painting of the chief depicted wearing the quilled and beaded shirt now in the National Museum of the American Indian, New York. Note the beaded dress worn by his wife. It appears to be the two-hide form (for the front and back) with the top edges turned down. Some of the beadwork follows this contour. *Oil painting by Richard Hook*

horse by the mid-late 18th century the Teton continued to move west beyond the Missouri River in three groups. The vanguard was the Oglala, who reached the forks of the Platte River and the Black Hills, followed by the Brulé on the upper portions of the Niobrara, White, and Bad rivers. The third branch, the Saone, lived along the tributaries of the Missouri, north of the Oglala and Brulé, as far north as Heart River. The Saone gradually divided into five subgroups by the early 19th century, thus giving the famous seven great bands which formed the Teton branch of the nation. These are:

- Oglala (Scatter One's Own)
- Brulé or Sicaugu (Burnt-thighs), divided with the Upper and Lower bands
- Hunkpapa (Campers at the horn or end of camp circle)

- Minneconjou (Plant at (or besides) the water)
- Sihasapa or Blackfeet, not to be confused with the Algonkian Blackfoot tribe
- Two Kettle or Ochenonpa (Two Boilings)
- Sans Arc or Itazipco (Those without bows)

All these large groups were further divided into smaller bands or camps called "tiyospaye." The Oglala had seven such bands at the time of the establishment of the reservations: Pushed Aside, Kiyuksa (Breakers of the law), Osages, Bad Faces, Untidy, Loafers, and Spleen, are the "gloss" terms. Repetitive terms such as "Kiyuksa" probably indicate shifting bands moving between tribes during the nation's western expansion. After the break up of the Great Sioux Reservation in 1889 the Teton bands were distributed as follows: the Oglala at Pine Ridge Reservation with a few (Milks Camp) at Rosebud; the Upper Brulé at Rosebud, a few at Pine Ridge; the Lower Brulé at the Lower Brulé Reservation, South Dakota; the Minneconjou, Sihasapa, Two Kettle, and Sans Arc were all settled on the Cheyenne River Reservation with some Sihasapa at Standing Rock; the Hunkpapa also at Standing Rock with a number at Ft. Peck, Montana and Wood Mountain, Saskatchewan. In 1868 the Teton were reported to number 21,215 within the U.S.

The total Sioux population including Santee, Middle, and Western Sioux within the U.S. have been given as 39,342 (1880), 31,192 (1930), 32,913 (1962), 103,255 (U.S. Census 1990); and for Canada 2,398 (1970) and 5,420 (1999).

FAR LEFT: John Grass or Charging Bear, Sihasapa (Teton) Sioux. An important chief of the Sioux at the Standing Rock Reservation in later life, here he wears an eagle feather warbonnet and trailer and holds a tobacco bag, pipe, and fan. Photograph Alexander Gardner, 1872.

LEFT: Running Antelope, Hunkpapa (Teton) Sioux, taken by photographer Alexander Gardner in 1872. He holds an eagle feather fan, pipe, and stem, and wears a highly decorated shirt with hairlock fringes. He was a great friend of Sitting Bull and welcomed him to Standing Rock Reservation in August 1881 after the leader's return from Canada.

LEFT: White Swan, a Chief of the Minneconjou (Teton) Sioux 1870. He wears a hair-lock fringed shirt and holds an eagle feather fan.

RIGHT: Pretty Bear, warrior Two Kettle (Teton) Sioux 1870. He wears tradecloth leggings with beaded strips.

FAR RIGHT: Running Bull, warrior Sans Arc (Teton) Sioux. Holding the same fan as Four Bears (see page 98). These Teton chiefs—with Pretty Bear, White Swan, and Red Feather—were part of a delegation of Minneconjous, Sans Arcs, and Two Kettles from Ft. Bennett under Major Randell to Washington D. C. in May–June 1870. Photograph (publisher) Gurnsey and Illingworth.

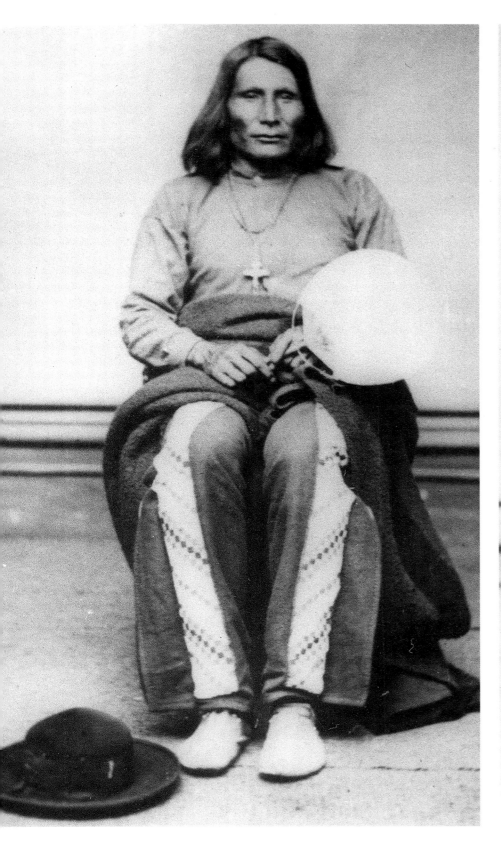

History

The first European mention of the Sioux was by Jean Nicolet in 1640, who heard of this nation the Natewessi living near the Winnebagos, although he probably did not go farther west than Green Bay. Radisson probably met them in the 1650s and after this the French from Canada were in frequent contact with them. In 1695 a Mdewakanton chief from Mille Lacs visited Montreal. The emigration of the Sioux from their original homes around Mille Lacs Lake in Minnesota about 1700 left those who still remained exposed to attacks from French traders and the incursions of the Ojibwas (Chippewas), who had been armed by the French and were expanding into areas which produced wild rice. By 1735 we hear of the Mdewakantons retreating down the Mississippi and the Tetons moving west to locate around Big Stone Lake. After the French and Indian War of 1754–63 the Sioux were now exposed to contacts by the British victors and were visited by the explorer Jonathan Carver in 1766. Under continuous pressure from the Ojibwa, the last bands of Sioux from Isanti (Knife Lake) were compelled to leave Mille Lacs about 1780, and the most important leader we hear about at that time was Wabasha (Red Headdress) who fought with the British during the American Revolution. By 1800 the Teton had moved west to the Missouri; the Yankton and Yanktonai were occupying the prairies between the James and Missouri; and the Sissetons moved in on the abandoned ground at Big Stone Lake, the Tetons fitting them out with stocks of horses. By this time it is evident the eastern branches of the Sioux were becoming dependent upon the trading facilities provided by the British and American fur companies and their adoption of tools, weapons, and utensils had modified native culture. However the eastern branches of the Sioux still had permanent villages of bark houses, and food still consisted of deer, elk, and bison; wild rice was still gathered and corn (maize) still planted.

The European Americans were largely responsible for the emigration of the Sioux from their original habitat through the acquisition of the horse and the supply of firearms to their enemies. The exact time when the Sioux came into possession of horses is unknown. Jonathan Carver, who visited them in 1766, makes no mention of horses although the Sioux were at war with Indians who did have horses. However, by the end of the 18th century all Sioux tribes had horses. Removal from their homes in the forests to life in the prairies and high plains wrought some radical changes to the habits and customs of these people who exchanged wild rice, berries, and fish for very nearly an exclusive diet of buffalo meat; gave up canoes for horses and bark houses for the light and transportable tipi of skins.

From the American Revolution until about 1810 almost continuous war existed between Wabasha's and Redwing's bands of Sioux and the Chippewas of Wisconsin, although the entire series of fights produced only limited casualties. However, with the transfer of the West to the United States following

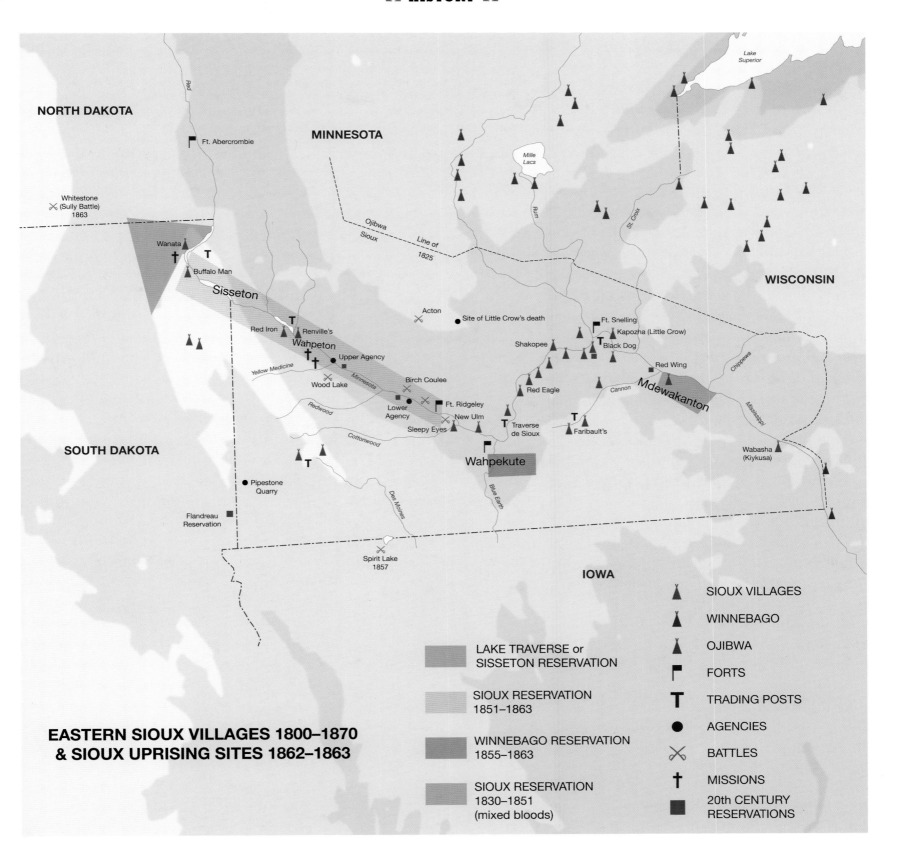

NORTH DAKOTA

Ft. Abercrombie

Whitestone
✕ (Sully Battle)
1863

Wanata

✝
T

Buffalo Man

Sisseton

Red Iron

T

Renville's

Wahpeton

✝✝

Yellow Medicine

Upper Agency

Wood Lake

Minnesota

MINNESOTA

Red

Ojibwa
Sioux

Line of
1825

Rum

Acton
✕

Site of Little Crow's death ●

Mille
Lacs

St. Croix

Lake
Superior

WISCONSIN

Ft. Snelling

Kapozha (Little Crow)

Shakopee

T

Black Dog

Red Wing

Chippewa

Birch Coulee
✕

Red Eagle

Cannon

Mdewakanton

Lower
Agency
●
✕

Ft. Ridgeley

New Ulm

Sleepy Eyes

Traverse
de Sioux

T

Mississippi

SOUTH DAKOTA

Redwood

Cottonwood

Faribault's

Wabasha
(Kiykusa)

Wahpekute

● Pipestone
Quarry

Flandreau
Reservation

Des Moines

Blue Earth

Spirit Lake
✕
1857

IOWA

EASTERN SIOUX VILLAGES 1800–1870
& SIOUX UPRISING SITES 1862–1863

LAKE TRAVERSE or
SISSETON RESERVATION

SIOUX RESERVATION
1851–1863

WINNEBAGO RESERVATION
1855–1863

SIOUX RESERVATION
1830–1851
(mixed bloods)

▲ SIOUX VILLAGES

▲ WINNEBAGO

▲ OJIBWA

⌐ FORTS

T TRADING POSTS

● AGENCIES

✕ BATTLES

✝ MISSIONS

■ 20th CENTURY
RESERVATIONS

the Louisiana Purchase of 1803, the Eastern Sioux (Santees) first official contacts with the U.S. began with Zebulon Pike's expedition of 1805–06, which established U.S. sovereignty over the area where British traders had continued to operate since the revolution. The Lewis and Clark expedition of 1804 had brought them into contact with the Western Sioux. The Oglala and Brulé were roaming west of the Missouri and the Saone along the river as far north as Heart River. The diaspora of the Sioux from the Minnesota villages was increasing the population of the emerging high plains Sioux whose camps absorbed these immigrants. Individuals and small bands could pass freely from subtribe to subtribe. However, these early American contacts do not appear to have succeeded in gaining the allegiance of the Sioux. The Santees fought on the British side in the War of 1812 when the British trader Robert Dickson attracted several chiefs to their cause including Wanata (Charger) the Yanktonai chief.

After the close of the war Wanata increasingly supported American interests. The Americans began to establish fur trade posts along the middle Missouri and through them direct trade with the Western Sioux. With direct contact came the first treaties by which the Indians were to recognize they lived within the territorial limits of the United States, acknowledging their supremacy and claiming their protection. In 1825 the Governors Clark and Cass met chiefs of all the bands from the Mississippi to Big Stone Lake at Prairie du Chien including Wabasha, Little Crow (Senior), Sleepy Eyes, Wanata, Redwing, and Shakopee. The same year General Atkinson and Major O'Fallon met representatives of the Teton, Yankton, and Yanktonai and concluded a treaty of friendship, and a separate but similar treaty was made with the Hunkpapa and Arikara. This was one of the most successful enterprises in which the

RIGHT: The battle of Tippecanoe, November 7, 1811. The followers of Tecumseh the Shawnee and his brother The Prophet had their village at Tippecanoe on the west bank of the Wabash River, Indiana. In the hope of raising more warriors to the cause of resisting American expansion in the mid-west, Tecumseh was in the south when the Americans under General William Henry Harrison, closing in on the village, were attacked by the Indians under the command of The Prophet. The Indians were completely defeated and Tecumseh's planned resistance abandoned. Tecumseh subsequently joined the British in the War of 1812 and received a regular commission and commanded 2,000 warriors of various tribes including Sioux. He died at the Battle of the Thames in Ontario, Canada refusing to retreat; he discarded his British uniform for deerskins, falling in front of his warriors on October 5, 1813. *Library of Congress*

BELOW: Lewis and Clark's expedition met the Yankton and Teton Sioux in 1804. *Library of Congress*

OPPOSITE BELOW, LEFT TO RIGHT: Col. Henry H. Sibley, commanded the Minnesota volunteers who defeated the Sioux in 1862; Gen. Alfred Sully led expeditions against the Sioux in 1863, 1864, and 1865; and Big Eagle, Santee Sioux chief who participated in most of the battles of the Minnesota Uprising in 1862.

27 ><

ABOVE: Red Iron, a Santee chief from the Upper Agency who helped arrange the release of white captives after the fighting at Wood Lake, Minnesota, 1862. Whitney photograph.

LEFT: Alfred Jacob Miller's view of the interior of Ft. Laramie in 1837. *Francis G. Mayer/Corbis*

government had engaged with the Indians since the explorations of Lewis and Clark.

After 1825 competition between rival fur companies began to make serious demands on the region's buffalo herds for their hides. The migration of the Hunkpapa and Sihasapa west of the Missouri resulted in the numbers of buffalo becoming increasingly erratic. In the 1830s the Oglalas and Brulés moved south into North Platte country, challenging the Pawnee, killing, burning their lodges, destroying crops, and stealing horses. In the 1840s there were serious clashes with the Crows and Shoshoni in the west and the Omahas in the south. By 1845 west-bound immigrant wagon trains were passing up the North Platte, thinning buffalo herds, and in the summer of 1849 increased white immigration moving along the Platte en route to the Californian gold fields brought cholera, which the Indians recognized as coming from the white man, and which they believed was spread deliberately. In 1849 the U.S. purchased Ft. John from the American Fur Company and installed a permanent garrison renaming the post Ft. Laramie. In September 1851 the first Laramie Treaty was agreed, with thousands of Indians in attendance from many tribes whose lands were being traversed by hordes of gold-seekers. The treaty defined tribal boundaries, and in return, Indians were to abstain from all depredations against whites through their country. However friction continued on the Oregon Trail in 1854 when Lt. Gratton's command was all but wiped out by Brulés. General Harney took his revenge at Ash Hollow, Nebraska the following year, attacking a camp of Brulés under Little Thunder while engaged in a parley, killing over 130 Indians.

The Eastern Sioux uprising of 1862–63 left more than 500 white settlers dead and launched a series of Indian wars on the northern plains, which

culminated in the Wounded Knee tragedy in 1890. The Eastern Sioux, the Santee tribes, had already a long association with whites. They had fought on the British side in the War of 1812, and had become dependent on the fur trade with some chiefs living in houses and dressing as whites. The treaty of 1851 signed at Traverse des Sioux and Mendota had seen the establishment of a reservation 20 miles wide and 120 miles long along the Minnesota River. The U.S. Government established the Upper Sioux Agency in 1853 to teach the Indians the ways of the white man, and its sister agency the Lower Sioux was located 30 miles downriver. There were approximately 7,000 Santee living on the reservation. In exchange the U.S. Government was to provide various provisions and cash annuities over a 50-year period to turn the Indians into self-sufficient farmers. However the Indians became more dependent upon government provisions which the government singularly failed to honor. Payments were late often, leaving them in debt to traders and mixed bloods. Further pressure in 1858 resulted in the northern strip of the reservation being ceded for additional cash and provisions. The crop failure of 1861, followed by a severe winter that delayed the annual spring hunts, was exacerbated by the failure of clerks to distribute provisions and cash in accordance with the treaty agreements. Open conflict broke out in August 1862 near Acton when some white settlers were killed by Indians from the Lower Sioux Rice Creek village. Perhaps because of their ties with the missionaries Stephen Riggs and

Thomas Williamson, most of the Upper Sioux refused to take part in the hostilities and many aided the whites during the short but bloody war. The war continued with attacks on Ft. Ridgely by Sioux under Little Crow, Mankato, and Big Eagle, but the siege was lifted, thus securing the north bank of the Minnesota River from further incursions, and Indian attacks on the south side were halted at New Ulm. After the successful defense of Ft. Ridgely and New Ulm, organized military efforts to defeat the Sioux were directed under Col. Henry H. Sibley with reinforcements. A setback at Birch Coulee when a burial party was attacked taught the whites the folly of entering into hostile country without a large and well-equipped force. Sibley built up his forces at Ridgely sending out offers of a truce after receiving evidence of division in the Sioux ranks. Chief Wabasha arranged for the safe release of several white and mixed blood captives. A force of over 1,600 men, including interpreter Riggs and scout Other Day, left Ft. Ridgely, and encountered Little Crow at Wood Lake. His defeat saw the end of organized warfare by the Sioux in Minnesota.

Following the fighting at Wood Lake, Wabasha, Red Iron, and the mixed blood Gabriel Renville organized the release of more whites. Approximately 1,200 Indians were taken into captivity as the starving Sioux surrendered. A military commission sentenced over 300 to death, reduced to 39 due to the intervention of Bishop Henry B. Whipple of Faribault with President Lincoln, and 38 were hanged at Mankato in December 1862. Those whose death sentences were commuted were later transferred from Mankato to prisons near

LEFT: Santee Sioux chief and daughters, c. 1864. Note: the steel pipe-tomahawk held by the man, his turban headdress, and beaded leggings. Photograph B. H. Gurnsey.

ABOVE: Eastern (Santee) Sioux woman Can-ku waste-win (Good Road Woman) c. 1864. Probably photographed at Ft. Snelling, Minnesota. Photographer Upton or Whitney.

LEFT: Execution of the 38 Santee Sioux Indians at Mankato, Minnesota, December 26, 1862. Among those executed were Tenazepa, Red Leaf, White Dog, Rdainyanka, Makatanajin, and Baptiste Campbell. Lithograph by Milwaukee Lith. & Engr. Co., 1863. *Library of Congress, Prints & Photographs Division LC-U.S.Z62-193*

Davenport, Iowa for three years, while uncondemned Sioux suffered the miserable winter of 1862–63 in a fenced enclosure near Ft. Snelling. After three years of distress the Sioux—mostly Mdewakantons and Wahpekutes—were moved to a reservation near the mouth of the Niobara River in Nebraska.

Little Crow himself escaped the punishment for the 1862–63 war as he and several bands fled to the Dakota prairies—probably Devil's Lake and in early 1863 he visited Ft. Garry in British Canada. He returned to Minnesota where he was killed on July 3, 1863, while picking berries near Hutchinson, Minnesota by Nathan and Chauncey Lamson. The Upper and Lower Sioux now roaming the Dakota prairies could still menace the Minnesota frontier and as a result two military expeditions were sent, one led by Sibley and the other by Gen. Alfred Sully from Ft. Randell on the Missouri. Sibley defeated the Sioux at Big Mound and Stony Lake, and Sully finally caught the Indians in the Killdeer Mountains of North Dakota in 1864 killing over a hundred. By 1866 Sioux raids on the Minnesota frontier gradually ceased. The Santees who had fled to the plains west of the Red River, mostly Sissetons and Wahpetons were gathered on reservations in 1867, at Devil's Lake (Spirit Lake) and Lake Traverse, South Dakota. A few crossed to Canada and never returned, such as Standing Buffalo's band in Saskatchewan, but a few small groups of Santees did

return to Minnesota in the late 1860s where Chief Good Thunder—who had protected white settlers during the war, purchased lands for his people in 1884. A few left Niobrara and settled at Flandreau in South Dakota in 1869 where they succeeded as farmers and some as producers of catlinite pipes from the nearby Piperstone Quarry (neutral ground for all tribes) in Minnesota.

Returning to the west, in 1861 gold was discovered in Montana. Immediately, the flow of gold-seekers instead of continuing westward turned north from Laramie, crossing the Powder River into the heart of Sioux buffalo hunting country. The U.S. Army took over protection of this so-called Bozeman Trail, building Forts Reno, Phil Kearney, and C. F. Smith to keep the trail open and protect gold-seekers. Ft. Phil Kearney was built in 1866 under the command of Col. H. B. Carrington with 2,000 men but was constantly harassed by Oglala and Minneconjou warriors. In December 1866 the Sioux successfully ambushed a relief force for a wood train detail and escort from Phil Kearney under Capt. Fetterman and in less than two hours all 90 men were killed, bodies stripped, scalped, and mutilated. However, the following summer a force under Maj. J. W. Powell again from Phil Kearney armed with modified Springfield breech-loading rifles and corraled in a strong positions with wagon bodies reinforced with logs and grain sacks gained significant revenge. Despite several charges hundreds of Sioux warriors failed to overrun the position and scores were swept away by the new firearms in the so-called "Wagon-Box Fight." While fighting along the trail continued the Treaty Commission and Sioux met again at Laramie agreeing the Second Laramie Treaty of 1868. Red Cloud, the Oglala chief in the Powder River country, refused to sign the treaty until the three forts were abandoned, and this done, he

ABOVE: Eastern (Santee) Sioux warrior Do-wan-sa or Tenazepa who was hanged at Mankato, Minnesota in December 1862 for his participation in the 1862 uprising. Photograph Martin's Gallery.

LEFT: Eastern (Santee) Sioux warrior Wa-kan-o-zhan-zhan (Medicine Bottle) photographed at Ft. Snelling, Minnesota in June 1864. He was executed in November 1865 for his part in the Minnesota outbreak of 1862. Photograph J. E. Whitney.

RIGHT: Little Crow, Mdewakanton (Santee) Sioux c. 1858. The third of a dynasty of chiefs of the Kapozha villages in Minnesota and was the principal leader of the Santee Sioux in the uprising of 1862–63. After his defeat at Wood Lake, he first sought protection of his kinsmen on the Plains. However, he returned to his old haunts and was killed in July 1863 near Hutchinson, Minnesota. Photograph J. E. Whitney.

FOLLOWING PAGE: Custer, fellow officers, and friends, Ft. Abraham Lincoln, 1873. He poses in front of his house, front row third left. Photograph O. S. Goff.

moved in and burned them before moving on to Laramie and signing as he had promised. The 1868 treaty defined the Great Sioux Reservation between the 104th meridian on the west and the Missouri River on the east, the 46th parallel on the north and 43rd parallel on the south. Among those who signed were representatives of the Oglala, Brulé, Minneconjou, Sihasapa, Two Kettle, San Arc, Hunkpapa, Yanktonai, and Santee. By 1870 more than half the entire Sioux people were living on reservations and drawing provisions from agencies. By 1869–70 peace had returned to Western Sioux country, and Chief Red Cloud and Spotted Tail made their first visits to Washington.

With Red Cloud and Spotted Tail now agency chiefs, new leaders were emerging such as Gall, Crazy Horse, and the spiritual leader among the Hunkpapa— Sitting Bull. Active hostilities resumed in 1871 during the survey for a railroad in an area still claimed by the Sioux. In 1872 there were attacks on the military at Pryor's Fork, Montana and on Ft. Abraham Lincoln. In 1873 rumors of gold in the Black Hills saw prospectors flood in as they had in California and Montana. In 1874 the government ordered an expedition into the Black Hills. Its chosen leader was Lt-Col George

ABOVE: Deputation of Brulé (Teton) Sioux Indians from the Whetstone Agency under Captain Poole to Washington D. C., May-June 1870. Front left/right Fast Bear, Spotted Tail, Swift Bear, and Yellow Hair.

ABOVE, LEFT AND RIGHT: Lt Charles F. Roe and the 2nd Cavalry built the memorial on the top of Last Stand Hill in July 1881, reinterring some soldiers' remains near the new memorial. Custer's body had been taken back to West Point Cemetery in 1877. These c. 1905 images show the memorial and gravestones. In 1991 the site was renamed Little Bighorn Battlefield National Monument and since then the memorials have been supplemented by those to the Indians who fell. *Library of Congress, Prints & Photographs Division, LC-USZ62-92286 (left) and LC-USZ62-121373 (right)*

RIGHT: Battle of the Little Bighorn: movement before the battle.

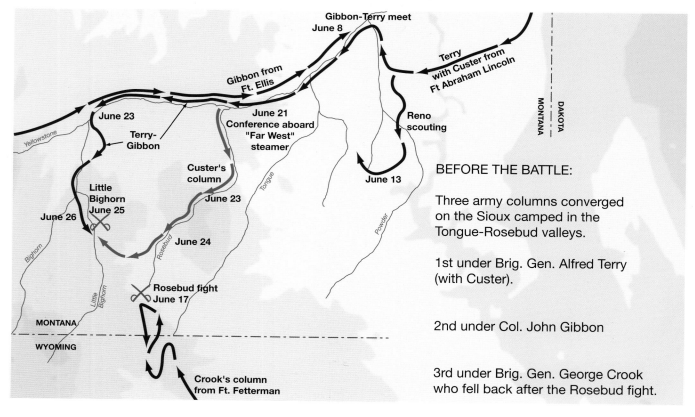

BEFORE THE BATTLE:

Three army columns converged on the Sioux camped in the Tongue-Rosebud valleys.

1st under Brig. Gen. Alfred Terry (with Custer).

2nd under Col. John Gibbon

3rd under Brig. Gen. George Crook who fell back after the Rosebud fight.

Armstrong Custer of the U.S. 7th Cavalry, a renowned Indian-hater who had already butchered Cheyennes under Black Kettle on the Wichita River, Oklahoma in November 1868. The expedition confirmed the presence of gold and the government concluded the only way to control the situation was to try to renegotiate the 1868 Laramie Treaty and offer the Sioux $6 million for the sale of the Black Hills. The Sioux promptly refused. The military response was to withdraw troops from the approaches to the Black Hills, allowing miners to pour in. Some Sioux retaliated by killing miners and leaving the agencies for the remaining buffalo-hunting grounds to the west in the Yellowstone, Powder, and Rosebud river country outside the control of the military.

The U.S. Army strategy for 1876 was to force these Sioux and their Cheyenne allies back to the agencies by encircling the Indians in south central Montana with three columns of troops: one commanded by Col. John Gibbon moving east from Ft. Ellis at Bozeman; the second under Gen. Alfred Terry (with Custer) moving west from Ft. Abraham Lincoln near Bismarck; and the third under Gen. George Crook moving north from Ft. Fetterman on the North Platte. The plan received a major setback when Crook's 1,300-strong column was defeated by Crazy Horse at the Rosebud fight on June 17, 1876, forcing him to withdraw and take no further part in the campaign. Terry met Gibbon on the Yellowstone at the mouth of the Tongue on June 8, and again on the steamer *Far West* near the mouth of the Rosebud. From there Custer on June 22 was despatched south down the Rosebud with orders to swing northwest to the forks of the Bighorn and Little Bighorn where Terry and Gibbon would be waiting. Custer's scouts tracked the horse hoof prints of the Indians west to a point now known as the "Crow's Nest," a ridge about

LEFT: Lt-Col. George Armstrong Custer (his rank in 1876), photograph taken during the Civil War when he rose to the rank of Brevet General. *Library of Congress, Prints & Photographs Division LC-DIG-cwpbh-03110*

FOLLOWING PAGE, LEFT: Totally misleading and inaccurate paintings of the Battle of the Bighorn appeared after the event. Custer's men died in groups in gullies, ravines, and bluffs on the east side of the Little Bighorn Valley over quite an area of ground. There are no high mountains near the battlefield as suggested in this fanciful image. Lithograph by Kurz & Allison, 1889. *Library of Congress, Prints & Photographs Division LC-USZC4-511*

FOLLOWING PAGE, RIGHT: Battle of the Little Bighorn: the battle, June 25, 1876.

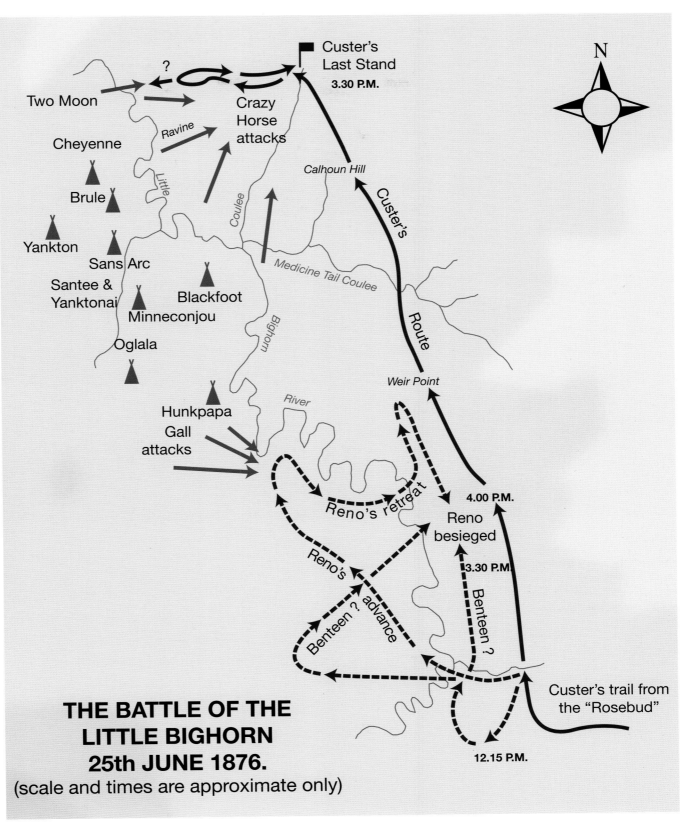

Custer's Last Stand
3.30 P.M.

Two Moon

Crazy Horse attacks

Ravine

Calhoun Hill

Cheyenne

Little

Custer's

Brule

Coulee

Yankton

Medicine Tail Coulee

Sans Arc

Route

Santee & Yanktonai

Blackfoot

Minneconjou

Bighorn

Oglala

Weir Point

River

Hunkpapa Gall attacks

Reno's retreat

4.00 P.M.

Reno besieged

3.30 P.M.

Reno's advance

Benteen ?

Benteen ?

Custer's trail from the "Rosebud"

12.15 P.M.

THE BATTLE OF THE LITTLE BIGHORN 25th JUNE 1876.
(scale and times are approximate only)

ABOVE: Little Bighorn battle site with the grave markers on Custer Hill. Custer's body was removed to West Point. M. G. Johnson photograph 1997.

15 miles from where a huge Indian village stretched for three miles along the Little Bighorn River. Custer's Crow Indian scouts were dismissed from further involvement and his Arikara scouts underestimated the number of Sioux and Cheyenne in the vicinity. However Custer, attacked without delay on the 25th, dividing his 7th Cavalry into three parties. Capt Frederick Benteen with companies D, H, and K was sent south to scout and report any Indian movements in that direction. Maj. Marcus A Reno led companies A, M, and G toward the southern end of the village. Custer himself with companies C, E, F, and I advanced north, some say,

following the line of a ridge running approximately parallel to the village scattered along the valley to his left. He apparently swung west over the crest of the ridge intending to cross the river and attack the northern end of the village. At what point he crossed the ridge or even if he reached the river remains in dispute. His column was repulsed and cut to pieces, although some troopers succeeded in retreating to a rise ever since known as Custer Hill and where a monument now stands. Custer was outnumbered and totally overwhelmed by fresh and better-armed warriors frantic to defend their women and children. Indian accounts of the battle dictated years later in

interviews with historians are often confused. With Custer died 215 men including his brothers Tom and Boston, a nephew, and a brother-in-law, with mutilated corpses found over a wide area. At the southern end of the village Maj. Reno's charge was halted when confronted by a huge number of warriors and retreated back across the river to be rejoined by Benteen's battalion to a site now known as Reno Hill, where fighting continued until June 26. Reno made no serious attempt to break out of this position, except for a few brave dashes to obtain water, and one of Benteen's officers—Thomas B. Weir—moved to a vantage point (which now also

bears his name, Weir Point) from where his troops caught glimpses of the Indians to the north through the smoke-haze of battle. Reno lost 47 killed and was relieved by Terry later on the 26th.

During the late summer and autumn of 1876 Crook returned to the field where his subordinates Col. Wesley Merritt (5th Cavalry) and Capt. Anson Mills (3rd Cavalry) gained victories over the Sioux at Warbonnet Creek, Nebraska and Slim Buttes, South Dakota respectively. In the later fight, old chief American Horse was killed. In October Col. Nelson held a meeting with Sitting Bull which ended in a running fight. Although Sitting Bull apparently did

ABOVE: Little Bighorn battle site. View west from Custer Hill towards the location of the huge Sioux and Cheyenne village. Note grave markers in foreground of fallen soldiers on that fateful day June 25, 1876. M. G. Johnson photograph 1997.

RIGHT: The horse "Comanche" was found on the Custer Battlefield two days after the battle of Little Bighorn (June 25th 1876) severely wounded. He had been the mount of Captain Myles W Keogh of the 7th Cavalry. He later became the mascot of the 7th Cavalry until his death when preserved by L. L. Dychein in 1891. He is on display in the Museum of Natural History, University of Kansas, Lawrence.

not take any part in the battle he had presided at a Sun Dance near the Rosebud Rover and had a vision of soldiers falling into his camp, taken as a prediction of the outcome of the forthcoming battle on the Little Bighorn, a few days later. During the winter of 1876–77 Cols. Mills and Mackenzie (4th Cavalry) harassed the Cheyenne and Sioux until by May most Indians had returned or surrendered to the agencies. Sitting Bull crossed into Canada with High Bear and Gall, but Crazy Horse surrendered in the spring of 1877: he was imprisoned and murdered. Gall and Sitting Bull returned to the Standing Rock Agency in 1881.

Yet another government commission was charged with the task of obtaining the Black Hills by a treaty change to the western boundary of the Great Sioux Reservation to which the agency chiefs Red Cloud, Red Leaf, Spotted Tail, and John Grass agreed. So the sacred Black Hills were ceded to the white man in 1877. Again in 1889 the Sioux were forced to surrender nine million acres of land and forced to accept six separate reservations in place of the single large one. The last of the buffalo were gone by 1884; the nomadic warrior-hunter culture had gone and the Sioux become farmers and ranchers. Their social and religious customs and their dress were to be discouraged and replaced by white man's dress and Christianity. The Western Sioux were no longer in control of their own destiny.

In 1889 the Sioux heard of a new cult, which

Warriors who killed Custer

The question of which Indian killed George A. Custer has interested generations of historians, and since there were no white survivors, they have turned for answers to the Indian accounts and interviews. However, in fear of retribution from the military, many of those accounts came from former warriors in their later years. Joseph White Bull (see also p.150) was sure he killed Custer for he had slain a soldier who wore a buckskin jacket as Custer often did. However, he was probably unaware that both Custer's brothers, also killed at the Little Bighorn, wore buckskin jackets and that several officers wore buckskin blouses.

Apparently only a handful of the hostile Indians had ever seen Custer and none knew Long Hair was on the field until after the battle. Custer, at his wife's request, had had his flowing locks trimmed short at Ft. Abraham Lincoln. Dewey Beard (see p.47) thought that Charging Hawk had killed the leader of the soldiers, and White Cow Bull claimed to have shot a man, whom he later heard called Long Hair, out of his saddle at the ford in the river adjacent to the huge Indian camp, but not to have killed him. However, his story confirms the troopers' halt in mid-charge and their shift from attack to defensive retreat, and ultimately the death of 215 cavalrymen.

Although Custer's body was found on the west slope of the ridge to which his troops retreated, it does not prove he was killed on that spot for if he was killed at the ford his body could have been carried there by the troops as they fell back. Other warriors who have claimed to have killed Custer include: Red Horse (Miniconjou), Flat Hip (Hunkpapa), Walks-Under-the-Ground (Santee), who was found in possession of Custer's horse, the sons of Inkpaduta (Santee, see p.149), and Fast Eagle (Oglala), who said he held Custer while Walking Blanket Woman, a girl warrior, stabbed him in the back. The showman Buffalo Bill even attempted to credit Sitting Bull.

When in 1909 the wealthy Philadelphian Rodman Wanamaker gathered the surviving warriors to a conclave on the Little Bighorn, he asked those present to prove who was Custer's killer. After days of deliberation in secret council the chiefs elected a 64-year old Southern Cheyenne named Brave Bear that distinction unanimously.

had derived from an earlier Californian cult, among the Paiute Indians of Nevada. Sioux pilgrims visited the cult leader Wovoka or Jack Wilson at the Walker River Reservation. On their return the Sioux described him as a messiah, having returned from heaven with a message of peace and reconciliation. However, the Sioux added their own, different interpretations which included the return of the buffalo and disappearance of the whites. They wore ritual clothes painted with symbols which would give the wearer protection against the white man's bullets. These Ghost Dance rituals—so-called because the Indians believed the ghosts of their ancestors would return—aroused great excitement on the Standing Rock Reservation. The agent James McLaughlin ordered the Indian police to restrict Sitting Bull whose followers had been Ghost Dancing for weeks. In a confrontation outside Sitting Bull's cabin on December 15, 1890, the old chief was shot dead by Red Tomahawk, an Indian policeman. The final event to this tragedy occurred when a band of dancers from Cheyenne River under Big Foot headed south to the Bad Lands, presumably to join Kicking Bear and Short Bull. The band was intercepted by Maj. Whiteside and escorted to Wounded Knee Creek on the Pine Ridge Reservation, where Big Foot's band was surrounded by troops from the 7th Cavalry, the unit cut to pieces 14 years before. On December 29, 1890, the soldiers, now under the command of Col. Forsyth, apparently heard a shot they believed came

LEFT: His Fights, Oglala (Teton) Sioux took part in the Battle of Little Bighorn in 1876. He wears a buckskin shirt with lazy-stitch beadwork. Published in 1908. Published in *The North American Indian* by Edward S. Curtis. [Seattle, Wash.] v.3. *Library of Congress, Prints & Photographs Division, Edward S. Curtis Collection, LC-USZ62-83595*

ABOVE: Dewey Beard or Iron Hail (Wazu Maza). Originally known as Beard he added "Dewey" to his name after meeting Admiral George Dewey, fresh from the Spanish-American War in Washington D. C. A Minneconjou (Teton) by birth he fought as a warrior at the Little Bighorn in June 1876. With the death of Sitting Bull's deaf-mute son, John in May 1955, Beard became the last Indian survivor of Custer's Last Stand. He died the following November, the last old patriarch of the fighting Teton Sioux. Shown here with his wife Alice in a postcard c. 1950.

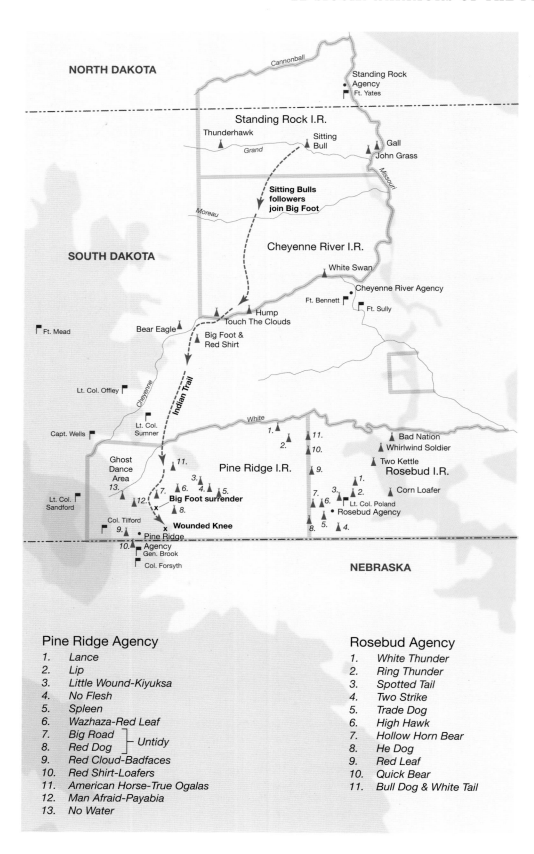

Pine Ridge Agency
1. *Lance*
2. *Lip*
3. *Little Wound-Kiyuksa*
4. *No Flesh*
5. *Spleen*
6. *Wazhaza-Red Leaf*
7. *Big Road* ⎤
8. *Red Dog* ⎦ *Untidy*
9. *Red Cloud-Badfaces*
10. *Red Shirt-Loafers*
11. *American Horse-True Ogalas*
12. *Man Afraid-Payabia*
13. *No Water*

Rosebud Agency
1. *White Thunder*
2. *Ring Thunder*
3. *Spotted Tail*
4. *Two Strike*
5. *Trade Dog*
6. *High Hawk*
7. *Hollow Horn Bear*
8. *He Dog*
9. *Red Leaf*
10. *Quick Bear*
11. *Bull Dog & White Tail*

from an Indian, and in the following confrontation killed over 300 men, women, and children, an action forever known as the Wounded Knee Massacre. The dead were buried in a common grave which remains today as a memorial to this event and the long sufferings of the Sioux people over the past two and a half centuries.

In 1887 the Congress passed The Dawes Act which allowed reservation lands to be allotted to individual Indians although this was not carried out until the turn of the century on the Western Sioux reservations. In the manipulation of the program many Indians exchanged their allotments so that their lands might adjoin those of their extended families consolidating native communities, so that the tiyospaye, the traditional Sioux social organization was perpetuated. These were mostly full-blood communities which became very quickly quite distinct from the more populous mixed-blood communities. Many Sioux, both Eastern and Western, had intermarried with French then American fur traders during the 18th and 19th centuries. About 1,000 mixed bloods were settled at the Whetstone Agency alone about 1870. Conditions on Sioux reservations were, and in places still are, characterized by poverty and inertia. By 1890 log cabins had replaced tipis; food, including beef, was distributed by the Indian agencies, but diet was poor resulting in widespread ill-health. Most Indians joined Christian denominations and native religious practices were barred or discouraged by government officials. However native language and some religious rituals survived among the tiyospaye communities such as those at Pine Ridge and Rosebud, and old warriors joined wild west shows and traveled to the eastern states and Europe performing dances and re-enacting battles for huge audiences.

FAR LEFT: Map of the Ghost Dance War, 1890, showing the Indian trail to Wounded Knee and Indian bands.

LEFT: Ghost Dance Shirt, Western Sioux (Teton) reported to be Oglala c. 1890. This shirt and many like it were made of muslin with painted designs representing the sun, moon, morning star, eagle, crow, magpie, and sometimes feathers were attached. The cult came originally from a Paiute prophet named Wovoka, whose Sioux disciples believed that the ritual would see the return of old practices and that, in trance-induced ceremonies, the painted devices on shirts and woman's dresses would protect dancers from the white man's bullets. In December 1890, 300 Indian men, women and children were killed by the Seventh Cavalry (Custer's old division) at Wounded Knee on Pine Ridge Reservation where Big Foot's Ghost Dance adherents had collected.

LEFT: The delegation of Western (Teton) Sioux chiefs to ratify the sale of lands in Dakota to the U.S. Government, December 1889. Photographed by C. M. Bell, Washington, D.C. *Library of Congress, Prints & Photographs Division LC-USZ62-95885*

Delegation of Sioux chiefs to Washington, October 14, 1888, under James McLaughlin.

Identification provided in 1937 by Vernon W. Wrenne, Rockford, Ill. with the help of Indian friends and a missionary to the Indians, Mr. Thomas Riggs of Pierre, S. D.

First row: Not identified

Second row, left to right:
1. Ugly Wild Horse
2. Pretty Eagle
3. He Dog
4. Good Voice
5. Quick Bear
6. Black Bull
7. Swift Bear
8. Ring Thunder
9. Two Strikes
10. Stranger Horse
11. Sky Bull
12. Red Fish
13. Yellow Hair
14. Eagle Horse
15. Thomas Flood (Interpreter)
16. Col. L. F. Spence (Agent at Rosebud)

Third row, left to right:
1. Sitting Bull
2. Stephen Two Bears
3. Bear's Rib
4. Thunder Hawk
5. High Eagle
6. Big Head
7. Mad Bear
8. Grey Eagle
9. Hairy Chin
10. Walking Eagle
11. High Bear
12. Fire Heart
13. John Grass
14. Gall
15. Louis Primeau (interpreter)
16. Major James McLaughlin (agent)

Fourth row, left to right:
1. Dog Back
2. Standing Soldier
3. Standing Elk
4. Little Hawk
5. Little Wound
6. Little Chief
7. Pretty Lance
8. High Pipe
9. Fast Thunder
10. No Flesh
11. American Horse (Wa-Si-Cun Ta-Shin-Ke)
12. Capt. George Sword (Indian Police)
13. Many Bears
14. Philip Webster (interpreter)
15. Philip Wells (interpreter)
16. Col. H. D. Gallagher (Agent Pine Ridge)

Fifth row, left to right:
1. Spotted Elk
2. Drifting Goose
3. Bowed Head
4. Standing Cloud
5. White Ghost
6. Crow Eagle
7. White Swan
8. Charger
9. Spotted Eagle
10. Swift Bird
11. Little No Heart
12. Narcisse Marcelle
13. Wm. Larabee
14. Philip Webster

Sixth row, left to right:
1. Wm. Carpenter (interpreter)
2. Fire Thunder
3. Bull Head
4. Big Mane
5. Medicine Bull
6. Wizi

Seventh row, left to right:
1. Mark Wells (interpreter)
2. Alex Rencontre (interpreter)
3. Joe Campbell (interpreter)

LEFT: Drifting Goose, Yanktonai Sioux chief whose village was located at Armadale Island near Mellette, South Dakota in the 1870s. *South Dakota State Historical Society*

RIGHT: Sioux men on horseback (group unknown), c. 1890. Mounted as if staged for a war party. Two horses have facemasks with horns and furs representing buffalo. Hanging below their mouths are human scalps. The Spanish who brought the horse to the American Southwest in the 16th/early 17th centuries also introduced metal armor. Along with the adoption of horses the Indians also adopted items of horse regalia including saddles, armor, and facemasks but in leather technology. Such armor survived until the early 19th century when firearms made them obsolete, but facemasks for horses survived for Indian pageantry and parades until the present day. The horse on the left has lightning painted down the legs. One warrior appears to hold an old society "bow lance." Photograph Keystone-Mast Company. *Library of Congress, Prints & Photographs Division LC-U.S.Z62-110873*

RIGHT: A Brulé (Western or Teton) Sioux war party, many men wearing war bonnets, on horseback in preparation for a staged raid on an enemy, December 26, 1907. *Published in* The North American Indian *by Edward S. Curtis. [Seattle, Wash.], Suppl., v.3, pl.85. Library of Congress, Prints & Photographs Division, Edward S. Curtis Collection, LC-U.S.Z62-46958*

RIGHT: Wahpeton and Yanktonai women and men, probably 4th July Powwow, Ft. Totten or Devil's Lake (Spirit Lake) Reservation, North Dakota, c. 1900. Note the beaded bandolier bags worn by one of the men, and the mass of beads and hairpipes worn by the women.

Cultural Traditions

The culture of the Santee or Eastern Sioux more closely resembled the Ojibwa than some of the more western groups of their own people. Generally they resided in the intermediate lands between the woodlands and tall-grass Prairie ecological zones relying on a food base of hunting, fishing, gathering, and horticulture. The first two activities were carried out by males; the last two by females. The Santee were never originally extensive buffalo hunters or sustained large-scale forays to the high Plains; moose and deer were their common quarry. The lakes and streams provided fish, often taken at night with the aid of birchbark and pitch torches. The most important wild foods were wild rice, maple sugar, and turnips. Women cultivated corn (maize), beans, squashes, pumpkins, and tobacco which would seem to indicate horticultural traits of antiquity, perhaps Mississippian. However wild rice areas became a source of continual dispute between the Santee and the Ojibwa with the latter continuing to gain ground at Sioux expense.

By 1763, at the close of the French and Indian War, the Santee still held most of what is now southern Minnesota. By 1800 the Sisseton and Wahpeton were becoming active middlemen in trade with their Yankton and Yanktonai relatives and became more closely tied and intermarrying with western relatives. By the early 19th century the Sisseton-Wahpeton were sharing prairie culture while the Mdewakanton-Wahpekute remained marginally woodlands. The former two groups followed the chase methods of the plains while the others, with limited horses, still hunted on foot.

The common dwelling of the Santee was a large gable-ended house with sloping roofs of birchbark, called "house-big." They also used conical or hemispherical cattail-mat or bark wigwams. The gable-ended house of bark had sleeping and lounging platforms about five feet wide about two and a half feet above the floor, extending around the inside, with floors covered with corn husk and cattail mats. Outside platforms served for drying corn and other vegetables. The Santee used canoes, usually the dugout variety. There were no exogamous patrilineal clans in the usual sense but the village orientation of the Santees tended to function similarly. The Santees closest to the Yankton also used the tipi, at least during the 19th century.

The principal weapons of the Santee were the long bow, ball-headed club and the gun-stock club. A triangular dagger contained in a chest-sheath was reported by the explorer Jonathan Carver in the 1760s. They also used wooden mortars of the woodland type to pound corn and large wooden bowls with carved animal or anthropomorphic heads at the edge were used in feasts. All Santee made and used birch-bark vessels, tumplines of moosehide, and barrel-shaped hide parfleches; and the Wahpeton and Sisseton made flat rectangular parfleches reminiscent of the Plains type. Wooden cradles with a protective head bow and solid wooden backs were similar to Ojibwa cradles and sometimes wrapping covers were decorated with porcupine quillwork.

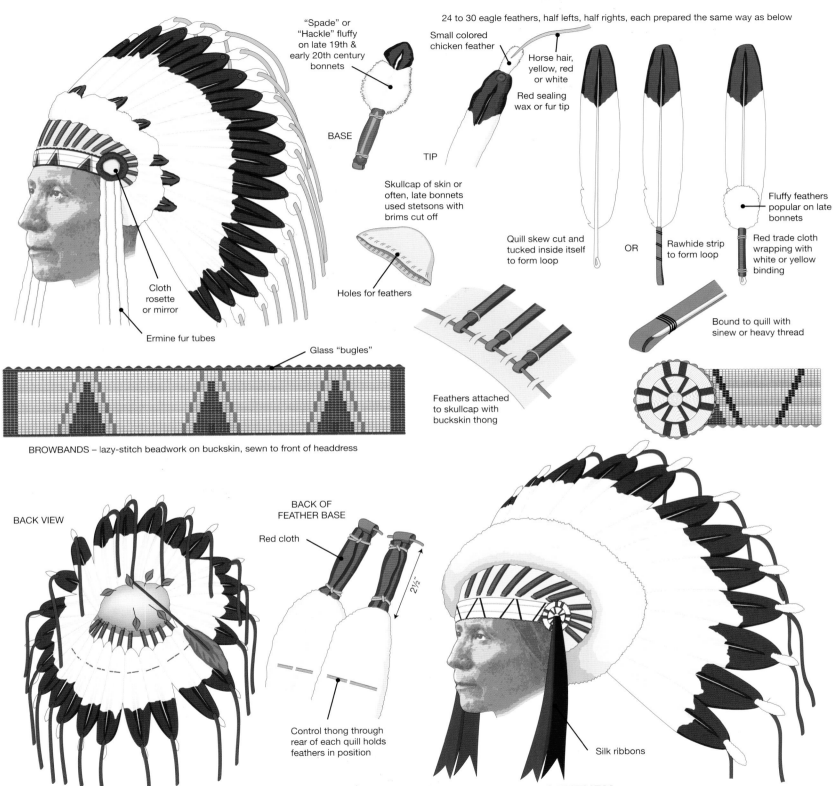

"Spade" or "Hackle" fluffy on late 19th & early 20th century bonnets

BASE

24 to 30 eagle feathers, half lefts, half rights, each prepared the same way as below

Small colored chicken feather

Horse hair, yellow, red or white

Red sealing wax or fur tip

TIP

Cloth rosette or mirror

Ermine fur tubes

Skullcap of skin or often, late bonnets used stetsons with brims cut off

Holes for feathers

Quill skew cut and tucked inside itself to form loop

OR

Rawhide strip to form loop

Fluffy feathers popular on late bonnets

Red trade cloth wrapping with white or yellow binding

Bound to quill with sinew or heavy thread

Feathers attached to skullcap with buckskin thong

Glass "bugles"

BROWBANDS – lazy-stitch beadwork on buckskin, sewn to front of headdress

BACK VIEW

BACK OF FEATHER BASE

Red cloth

2½"

Control thong through rear of each quill holds feathers in position

Silk ribbons

TYPICAL DETAILS OF LATE 19th – EARLY 20th CENTURY EAGLE FEATHER HEADDRESS OR "WAR BONNETS" OF THE SIOUX

The position of band chief was hereditary among the Santee, passing from father to eldest son. Each chief appointed a head soldier or "akicita" who acted as a policeman for the village. In times of war he was assisted by other akicita selected from various warrior societies. Separate "hunt chiefs" were selected by the councils during the duration of hunting parties and were often assisted by the akicita. Groups of akicita formed tiyospaye or "soldier lodges." These groupings both social and military repeated among all the various Sioux groups. After 1763 the Santee incorporated white traders into their kinship networks and used these ties to gain an advantage in their commercial dealings with whites. The fur trade brought dependence on European tools, including guns, traps, and axes. Trade cloth, beads, and metal objects replaced native technology which were available to the Santee from British sources at Ft. Garry in Manitoba, but after 1819 they became increasingly subordinate to the U.S. who created military garrisons on ceded lands. Santee games included snow snake (spears thrown along a snow track), Lacrosse, and Shinny. Gambling was popular with both men and women.

What we know of Santee dress comes from objects in museums made during the 19th century such as the collection made by Nathan Sturges Jarvis between 1833 and 1836, now in the Brooklyn Museum, New York. Women's buckskin dresses were probably the so-called "strap dress" having two straps at the shoulders and possibly the rare "side-fold" dress, a few specimens of which survive from the eastern margins of the parklands but without documentation. The surviving men's ceremonial shirts (deer, elk, or antelope) are probably Sisseton, Wahpeton, and Yanktonai examples, i.e. from the more western groups. They are rather close fitting and decorated with woven or appliqué porcupine

quillwork, sometimes bird quillwork, and occasionally pierced decoration. Later cloth shirts with beadwork or ribbonwork came into use. Men wore breechcloth between the legs and hung over the belt, and front seam leggings (both buckskin and cloth) with large flaps projecting out above the knee. Santee women also wore the two-piece woodland-style costume consisting of a wrap-around skirt and loose blouse often ornamented with a profusion of silver broaches, beadwork or ribbon appliqué. Floral beadwork similar to the Ojibwa and Winnebago forms became popular with the Santee during the 19th century but often incorporating birds and animals into the designs. The Santee used several types of moccasin construction including the old Woodland single front seam style and the vamp form which has a beaded tongue, "U" shaped, over the instep with many variations. Headdresses included the porcupine and deer-tail roach, finger-woven sash turbans, otterskin fillets with eagle feathers and hoods. The Santee and Yankton are noted for their production of catlinite pipe-heads from the famous pipestone quarry.

The culture and economy of the Middle or Wiciyela Sioux was heavily influenced by the Missouri River horticultural tribes such as the Hidatsa and Arikara and rested on a base of river-bottom gardening, hunting, and fishing. Great tribal bison hunts took place twice a year, in mid-summer and late fall. These hunts often took both Yankton and Yanktonai far west of the Missouri and the Yankton made periodic trips to the Black Hills of South Dakota to secure tipi poles. Bison, elk, deer, and antelope were taken throughout the year by small hunting parties closer to home. Fishing—by means of large weirs—and gathering turnips, chokecherries, and other wild foods provided additional nutrition. Both tribes practiced

LEFT: Double trailer eaglefeather warbonnet once mistakenly believed to have belonged to Red Cloud and once used on the same mannequin as the famous shirt (see page 67) at the Buffalo Bill Historical Center, Cody, Wyoming. The beaded browband suggests Shoshoni work, early 20th century.

ABOVE: James Lone Elk Western Sioux man c. 1900. Wearing an eagle feather "warbonnet" which became so popular with Sioux men during the last part of the 19th and early 20th centuries, particularly when working in Wild West shows. Eagle feather heraldry was endemic among the Plains Indians and bonnets were being recorded by white artists by the 1830s. They became a symbol of the American Indian and adopted by many tribes who never wore these headdresses originally. Oddly the Sioux rarely use them today perhaps in honor of their warrior forefathers. Only men who have served in the military are entitled to wear them today. Photographer Heyn. *Library of Congress, Prints & Photographs Division LC-USZ62-55850*

horticulture with women raising various varieties of maize, squash, and beans, but farming was not as intensive as with the Santee.

The Yankton and Yanktonai both used the skin tipi of the three-pole foundation type, and sometimes poorer families used a skin-covered wikiup. Earthlodges, abandoned by the Arikara, were also used and probably constructed by some bands as the sites of a number of earthlodge villages are known to have been Yanktonai. Drifting Goose's village at Armadale Island, South Dakota was known to have earthlodges in 1863. Bullboats, round and rowboat-shaped, were also used by the tribes to cross the James and other rivers of the tall grass prairie country. For both hunting and warfare the Middle Sioux employed the short bow (sinew-backed) as it was adapted for equestrian use; shields and Woodland-style ball-headed and gun-shaped warclubs were used. The Yanktonai are said to have made clay pots and willow baskets in the manner of the Arikara.

Fringed buckskin shirts were worn by both Yankton and Yanktonai such as an example in the National Museums of Scotland said to have belonged to Chief Wanata. Shirts and leggings were decorated with porcupine and bird quilled strips, painted with stripes, dots, and battle scenes (pictographs). A number of examples of warrior shirts survive in European and North American museums but almost all lack precise tribal attribution but probably were made on the eastern and northern borders of the Great Plains during the first half of the 19th century. No doubt a number are Yanktonai, Sisseton, and Wahpeton and collected from chiefs and traders on the Missouri waterway. Some shirts show European influences in the construction details; others have a clearly revised art style in the painted figures of equestrian or unmounted warriors indicating Euro-American exposure.

The Teton or Western Sioux are fairly recent migrants to the plains region. After leaving their original homeland within the present state of Minnesota they were moving west to the Lake Traverse area by 1750 and to the Missouri River by about 1775. Sometime later the southern Teton, the Oglala, and the Brulé crossed the Missouri around the mouth of the White River into the high plains short-grass country gathering vast herds of horses and changing to a nomadic hunting culture with the buffalo (American bison) the mainstay of their economy, supplemented by deer and pronghorn antelope.

By the late 18th century the Oglala territory extended from the Platte to the Cheyenne River including the Black Hills, and the Brulé were to the east. From 1771 to 1781 smallpox decimated the Arikara with remnants moving north allowing a second migration of Sioux to cross the Missouri, called Saone, to settle along the tributaries of the Missouri from Cheyenne River north to Heart River. This group subsequently divided into five large bands (large enough to be regarded as minor tribes), the Minneconjou, Hunkpapa, Sans Arc, Blackfeet, and Two Kettle. By the mid-19th century the Oglala, Brulé, and Minneconjou lived in and beyond the

Black Hills, drawn westward by the abundance of bison in the Powder and Yellowstone river country while the remaining Teton were more dependent on the presence of white traders, military establishments, and agencies along the Missouri River.

The characteristic local group of the Teton was the tiospaye or camp, who were essentially extended bilateral and bilocal kin groups. Each of these tiospaye was headed by one or more chiefs. A number of such tiospaye made up a band (see under Teton p.6). Bands such as the Oglala elected four "shirt weavers" or chief councillors. The instructions of the council were carried out by four Wakicun (or head councillors) and the akicita, members of the warrior or soldier societies. The Teton had an elaborate system of male warrior societies scattered through all the great bands, such as the Kit Foxes, Crow Owners (who had a special type of dance bustle), Badgers, Bare Lance Owners, White Horse Riders, Owl Feather Headdress, Miwatani or Mandan, and Strong Hearts. The Silent Eaters, of which Sitting Bull was a member, was confined to the Hunkpapas. These societies were a fighting group and fought as a unit when possible. Each had its own chiefs, heralds, or criers. Another type of organization—but mystical in character—was the dream society, made up of men who shared a similar dream, usually an animal from which they derived power. Principal of these were elk and buffalo. The elk provided sexual power and long life.

Both men and women wore their hair in two braids, one each side of the head. Men often wrapped their braids in otter skin or red cloth shrouding, while women fastened elaborate quilled or beaded bobs to the ends. Men's shirts were elaborately decorated with quilled strips over the shoulders, and arms with fringes of human or horse hair and neck flaps in rectangular or triangular

LEFT: Teton (Western) Sioux woman and child, c.1885, probably at Rosebud or Pine Ridge Reservation, South Dakota. Both wear Plains Indian metalwork on belts, decorated moccasins, and dresses made from trade cloth. The vertically strung bone "hairpipes" were also obtained from white traders and are still popular today with Indian women at powwows.

RIGHT: Stampede, Najinca, Brulé (Western) Sioux wears a war bonnet and bone "hairpipe" breastplate. His wife and daughters all wear selvedge-edged trade cloth dresses with dentalium shell decoration. His wife wears beaded leggings, moccasins, and German silver hairplates on her belt and drop. Stampede was born in 1859. J. A. Anderson photograph c. 1900. *Library of Congress, Prints & Photographs Division LC-USZ62-101271*

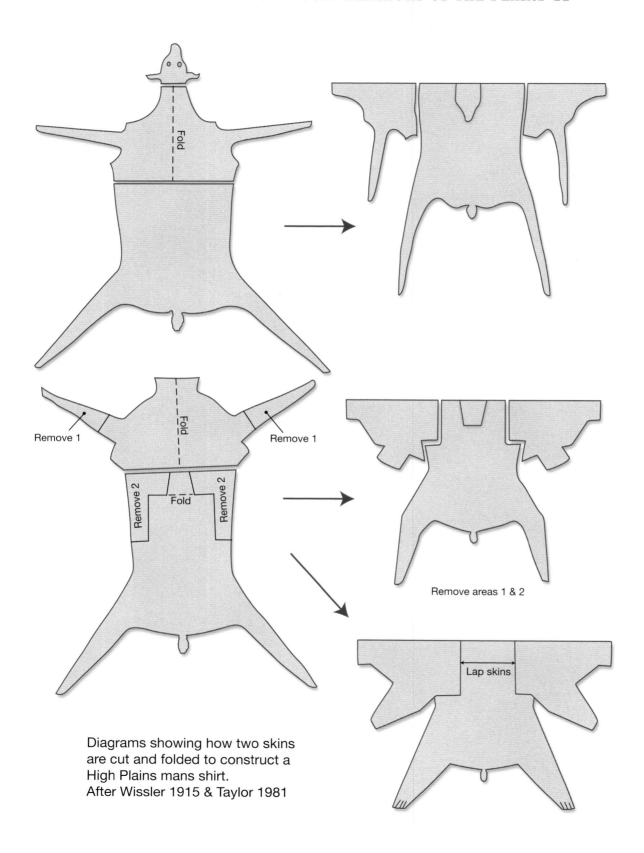

LEFT: Diagrams showing how two skins are cut and folded to construct a High Plains shirt after Wissler 1915 and Taylor 1981.

RIGHT: Man's shirt, Western Sioux, c. 1865. This magnificent shirt was worn by several Sioux chiefs in Washington: Red Cloud, American Horse, Touch-the-Clouds, and Little Big Man were all photographed wearing it (see photograph of Red Cloud on page 153). The buckskin is painted blue (upper area) and yellow (lower area). The beaded strips are heavily fringed with hair-locks. The shirt is now in the Buffalo Bill Historical Center, Cody, Wyoming.

Remove 1

Remove 1

Fold

Remove 2

Fold

Remove 2

Remove areas 1 & 2

Lap skins

Diagrams showing how two skins are cut and folded to construct a High Plains mans shirt.
After Wissler 1915 & Taylor 1981

LEFT: Western Sioux (Teton) man's shirt c. 1880. Constructed of two or three skins, front, back, and arms. The shirt has shoulder strips in beadwork using the lazy-stitch (or lane-stitch) technique. There is also a truncated "vee" shaped neck flap and hair-lock fringing. The upper body is painted blue-green and the lower area yellow which is typical of Western Sioux shirt of this and earlier periods. Buffalo Bill Historical Center, Wyoming.

RIGHT: A remarkable Western Sioux war shirt of buckskin, porcupine-quilled, and beaded strips and decorated with hair locks. The shirt was reported to have been collected from the Brulé Chief Spotted Tail (Sinte Gleska) by 2–Lt. Charles G. Sawtell at Ft. Laramie in 1855. Spotted Tail was born about 1823 and rose to rank of Chief by leading successful war parties. He was probably at the Gratten fight of August 1854 during troubles on the Oregon Trail with Conquering Bear's Brulés and again at Ash Hollow when General Harney took his revenge. He signed the 1868 Laramie Treaty and later became a leader of the Brulés at the Rosebud Agency where he was murdered by Crow Dog in 1881. A successful college (now a university) on the present day Rosebud Reservation perpetuates the old Chief's name, Sinte Gleska College. *Richard Hook, National Museum of the American Indian, Smithsonian Institute*

shapes. Such shirts, particularly the early pre-1870 specimens were replete with warrior and protective symbolism. Large trade beads (ponybeads) obtained from the white traders were often used in conjunction with quills to border strips, and after about 1870 such work was done in the smaller seed beads in increasingly complex geometrical designs.

Moccasins were of the rawhide-sole plains type, although earlier styles, shared with the Santee, were probably the ancient center-seam woodland form. Many moccasins were fully beaded in geometrical designs. Hairpipes were popular with men and women after 1870. Made of shell or animal bone in tubular shape they could be strung together vertically for women and horizontally for men. White traders had originally brought shell hairpipes and dentalium shell to the plains, but the larger bone hairpipes became extremely popular for ceremonial dress and continue to be popular for dance dress today.

The earliest known deerskin dress form used by the Sioux women was the so-called "strap dress," the body, covering to about mid-leg, was held over the

RIGHT: Wanata, Yanktonai Sioux Chief and trader, painted by Charles Bird King in 1826 based on an original by James Otto Lewis painted at the Treaty of Prairies du Chien of 1825. A chief's dress reported to have belonged to the celebrated Sioux Chief Wanatah (Charger) was given to a trader named Walker, who in turn passed it to a well-known trader, William Laidlaw of the Columbia Fur Company, and via his friend, a Mr. Rutherford, was sent to Scotland by 1837. The costume comprising a shirt, leggings, and other items is now in the National Museums of Scotland, Edinburgh, who acquired it in 1843.

FAR RIGHT: Man's shirt attributed to Wanata, before 1844. Antelope or deer skins, decorated with quillwork strips, discs, tradecloth, and human hair. Painted fighting scenes showing horse-mounted and pedestrian warriors in red, brown, yellow, green, and purple. Length 134cm. *National Museums of Scotland, Edinburgh, 1942.1a.*

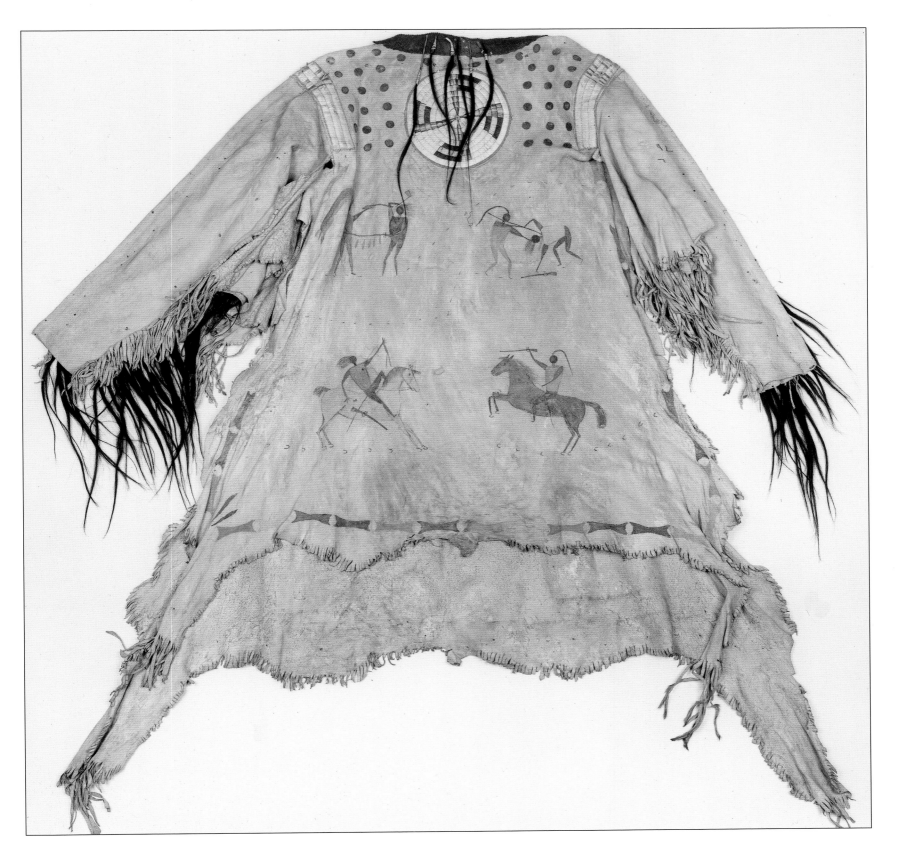

SIOUX: WARRIORS OF THE PLAINS

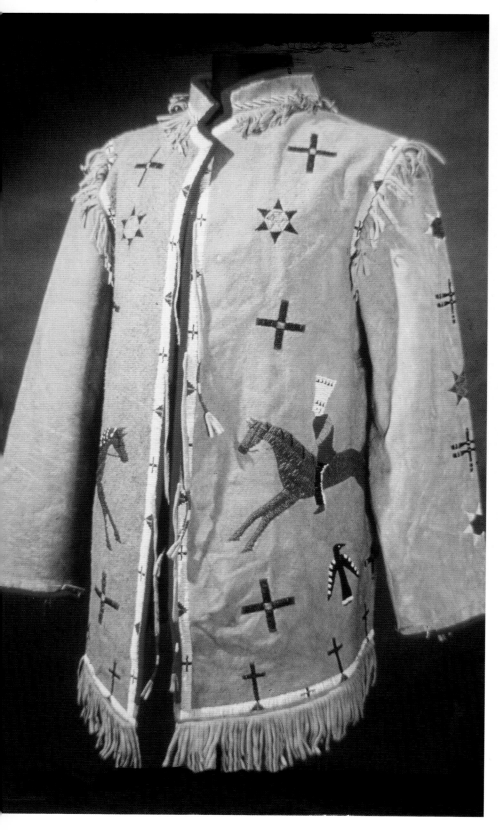

LEFT: Scouts jacket, Sioux c. 1890. A completely Euro-American style buckskin jacket beaded with warrior and geometrical designs. Such items were worn by army scouts and mixed bloods since two cultures are represented. *Courtesy University Museum of Cambridge UK Owen Collection*

ABOVE: Warrior shirt, early 19th century. Upper Missouri River type, probably Sioux (back view). This is an untailored shirt formed with three hides (front, back, and arms). The use of fully intact animal skins was believed by Plains Indians to bestow upon the wearer the spiritual power of that animal. Most of these early shirts are undocumented, and many defy tribal attributions. The quillwork (porcupine and bird?) bands are in five lanes with a further outside lane of blue "pony" or "pound"

72

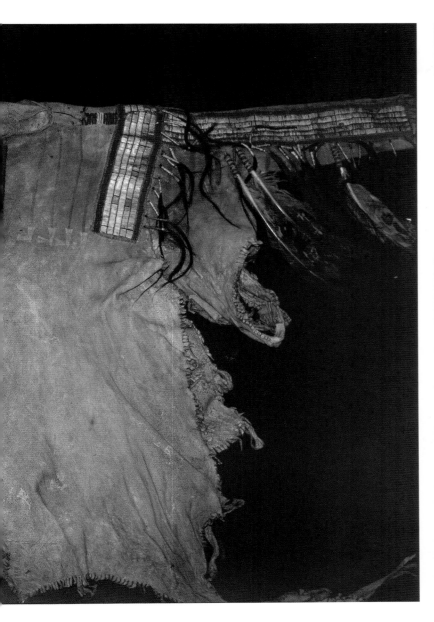

beadwork. The quillwork designs to both arms and shoulders have orange-yellow color areas bordered with dark edges (originally black?), a style noted on a number of similar examples. Four pipes are drawn vertically on either side of the red stroud cloth neck flap which is also edged with blue pony beads. The edges of the quilled strips have quill-wrapped hair fringes and eagle feathers. *Courtesy Manchester Museum, Salford Collection #09322/500*

RIGHT: Warrior shirt, c. 1870, Western (Teton) Sioux. Typical buckskin shirt with painted areas (blue, green, and yellow) of the third quarter of the 19th century. Note the double "vee" detail on the neck flap, a detail shared with the so-called Red Cloud shirt, and the wide beaded lazy-stitch shoulder strips. *Courtesy National Museum of the American Indian*

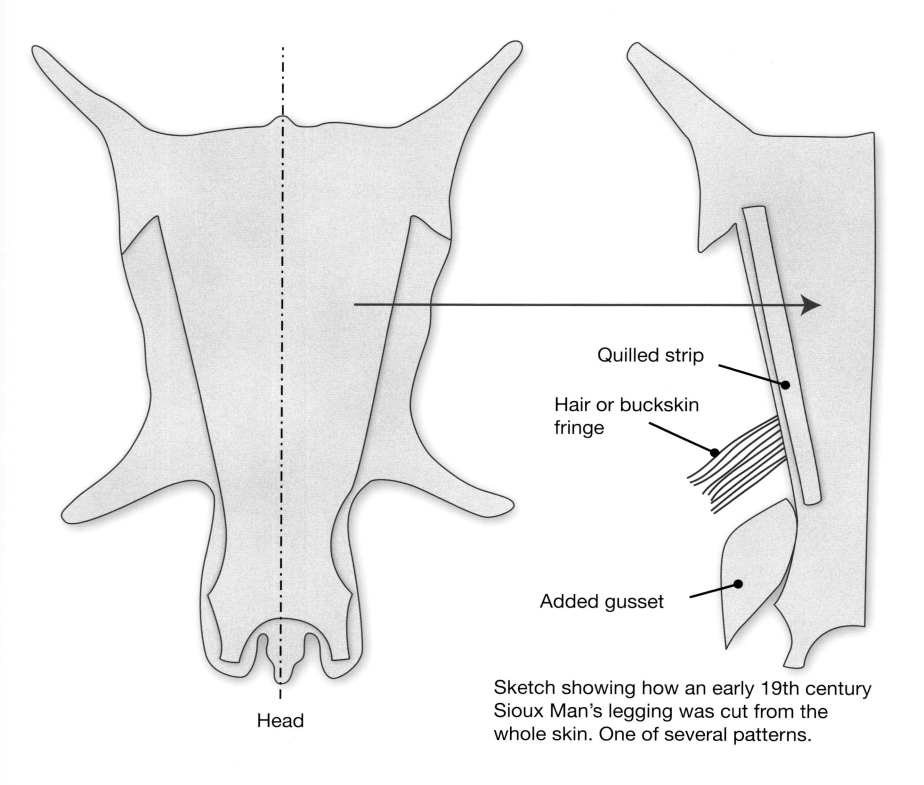

Quilled strip

Hair or buckskin fringe

Added gusset

Head

Sketch showing how an early 19th century Sioux Man's legging was cut from the whole skin. One of several patterns.

shoulders by a strap each side. Another early form was the "side-fold dress" perhaps derived from folded robes. However, these forms had disappeared from the dress of Western Sioux women by the 1840s, although strap dresses were still used by the Eastern and Middle Sioux until their time. The two and three-skin dress became the typical Western Sioux form after 1830. The two-skin type, with a fold back at the shoulder, was modified to a three-skin with a seam approximating the underside of the arm. These dresses were embellished with bands of blue and white ponybeads and elk teeth. A later revision indicator has the seam of the shoulder skin and body skin sewn much lower, a form which persists until today. For a time in the 1880–1910 period trade cloth dresses were also popular.

The tipi was the typical dwelling of the Teton, originally of buffalo hides over a framework of poles, with an inner liner extending about four feet high around the interior of the lodge. Thde poles were dragged by horses, or formed travois or platforms for tipi covers and other items, when moving camp. The Sioux also kept records of important events in their tribal or personal history by means of so-called winter counts which were painted on bison hide—or later on canvas or muslin—recording a principal event for each year. Plains Indian art developed through the 19th century from simple human and animal forms with no Euro-American influences to highly sophisticated images of complex scenes showing warriors in full dress, holding shields and weapons in battle displays.

Shields were made of fire-hardened buffalo bull hide and painted with sacred designs based upon a man's vision. When not in use the shield was protected by a cover of tanned hide. Bows were generally of ash, about 3.5ft long for use on horseback and often double-curved and sinew-

LEFT: Sketch showing how an early 19th century Sioux man's legging which is cut from the whole skin. One of several patterns.

ABOVE: Men's leggings, early 19th century. Upper Missouri River type, possibly Sioux. Each legging consists of a folded animal skin and an added gusset. Quillwork bands in five lanes with some blue and white pony beads. The colored orange-yellow areas with the dark borders link these leggings to other garments from the Missouri River or adjacent Plains region and of the early 19th century period. *Courtesy Weston Park Museum, Sheffield. Wharncliff Collection*

backed. Arrows were also of ash about 25 inches long with stone or bone points later replaced with points of hoop iron or other Euro-American metal. Long lances were used for buffalo hunting or war and many were also used as ceremonial regalia for men's societies. Clubs were stone-wrapped in rawhide attached by a short buckskin cord to a wooden handle which was beaded. Many of the later type were used as dancers' regalia.

The Sun Dance was the most important public religious ceremony, held each summer when bands came together to celebrate tribal unity and pray for the return of the buffalo and world renewal. Versions of the rite are still performed on many reservations today.

The Western Sioux also popularized the eagle feather "warbonnet," which originally had strong connections with war symbolism but which later simply became an ethnic badge for all American Indians.

LEFT: Eastern (Santee) Sioux boy Ma-zo-oo-nie? (The Little Bird Hunter) c. 1864. The translation is incorrect. The buckskin leggings are the rare front-seam type known to have been made by the Western Woodland and Prairie tribes. The boy wears a roach with two eagle feathers.

CENTER LEFT: Red Deer and baby c. 1900. Western Sioux woman holding a baby in a fully beaded cradle. Occasionally Sioux cradles were mounted on boards similar to their friends the Cheyenne. A few Cheyenne lived on the Pine Ridge Reservation and intermarried with the Oglala. Photographer Heyn and Matzen. *Library of Congress, Prints & Photographs Division LC-USZ62-55818*

FAR LEFT: Man's buckskin legging, showing the beadwork designs in appliqué stitch. Wahpeton (Santee) Sioux, collected from the Canadian Wahpeton, c. 1920. *Rymill Collection No. 30865 Cambridge University Museum of Archaeology and Anthropology*

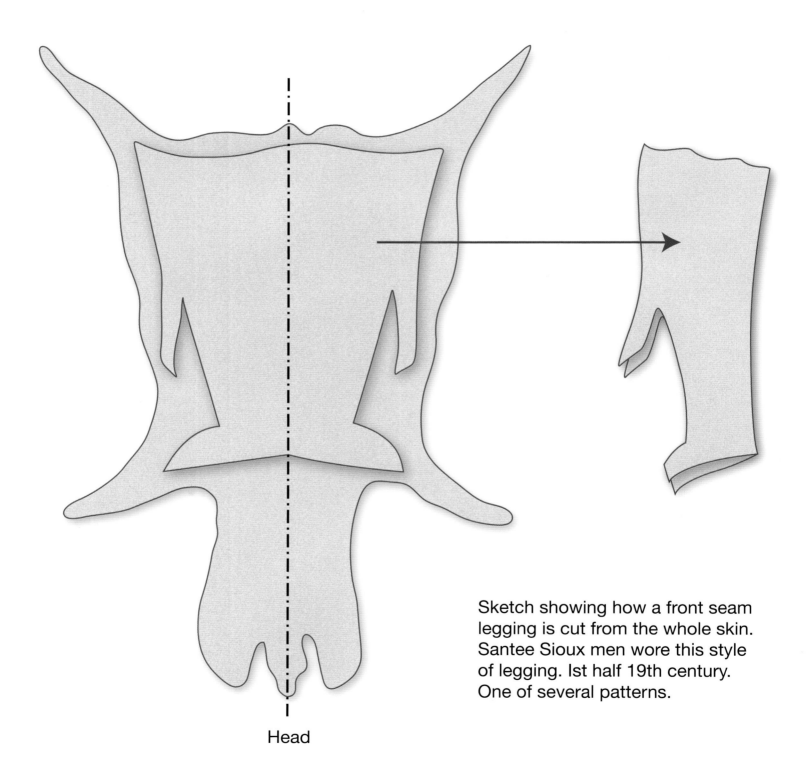

Sketch showing how a front seam legging is cut from the whole skin. Santee Sioux men wore this style of legging. Ist half 19th century. One of several patterns.

Head

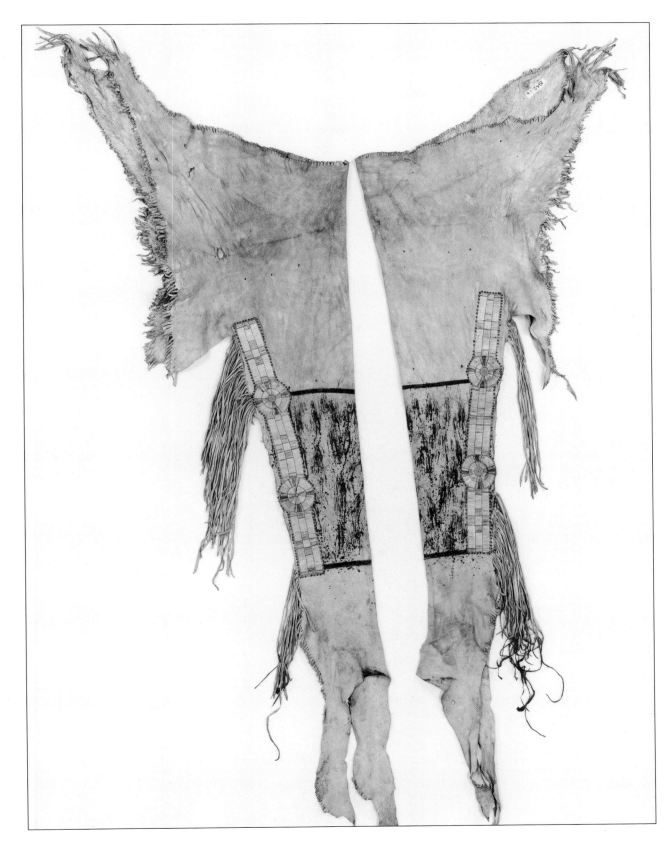

FAR LEFT: Sketch showing how a front seam legging is cut from the whole skin. Santee Sioux men wore this style of legging. First half of 19th century one of several patterns.

LEFT: Man's leggings, probably Yanktonai Sioux, attributed to Wanata c. 1830. Antelope skin (?), paint, blood (?), and three-lane quillwork on strips. *National Museums of Scotland, Edinburgh, 1942.b.c.*

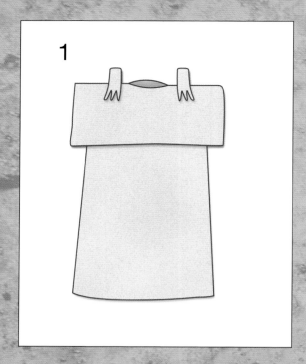

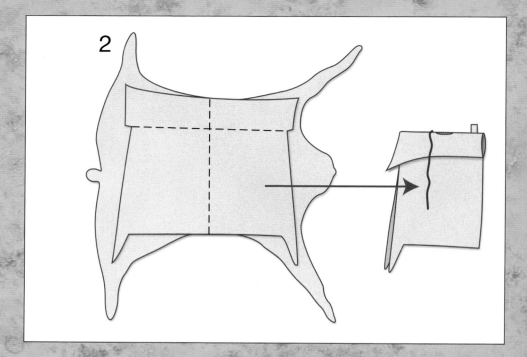

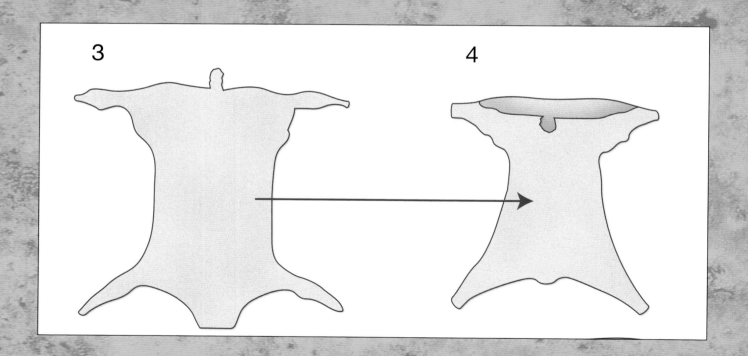

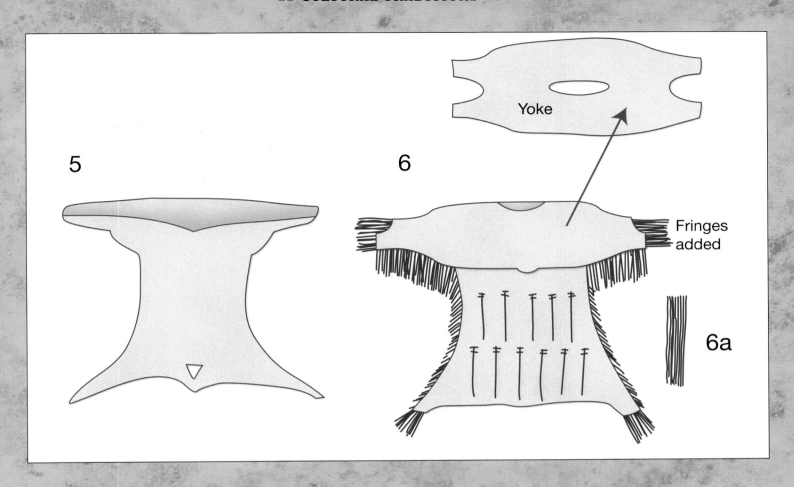

Yoke

Fringes added

6a

Sioux women's dresses

1 Strap dress (Santee and Yanktonai)
2 Rare side fold dress
3 Contour of elk skins (two required—
   one front and one back)
4 Two-skin form with fold back; early
   19th century
5 Three-skin form mid-19th century
6 Three-skin form with Yoke and low
   seam
6a Modern long fringes
7 Trade cloth dress; late 19th–early 20th
   century

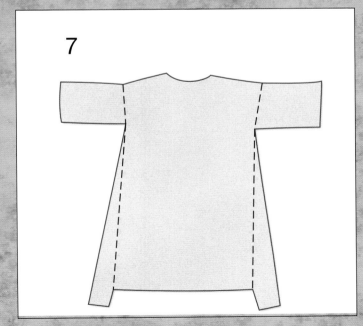

RIGHT: Western Sioux woman's dress c. 1880. Constructed of three skins, front, back, and yoke which is heavily beaded with a blue background. Sometimes the yoke was separate. The model also wears a concho belt with German silver conchos and hairpipe necklace. Buffalo Bill Historical Center, Cody, Wyoming.

FAR RIGHT: Woman's dress, Sioux 1914. A three-skin (elk?) buckskin dress with a large yoke joining the body lower compared with older three-skin dresses. The whole of the yoke area is solidly beaded in late style geometrical and realistic designs. The "U" shaped device at the lower center of the bodice area is a symbolic tail of the upper hide and a female reference. Sacred Circles Exhibition, London 1976.

FAR LEFT: Two Oglala (Western) Sioux girls on horseback, wearing beaded dresses and moccasins. Oglala women were experienced horse handlers. c. 1907. Published in *The North American Indian* by Edward S. Curtis. [Seattle, Wash.] suppl., v.3, pl. 96. *Library of Congress, Prints & Photographs Division, Edward S. Curtis Collection, LC-U.S.Z62-106991*

LEFT: Slow Bull's wife, Oglala (Teton) Sioux c. 1908. She wears a bone hairpipe necklace and a trade cloth dress decorated with dentalium shells. Her earrings are also made of dentalium shell. Her husband, Slow Bull was an Oglala (Teton) Sioux born in 1844 who became a subchief in 1878. Curtis provided a short biography of him in *The North American Indian* Volume III. *Corbis*

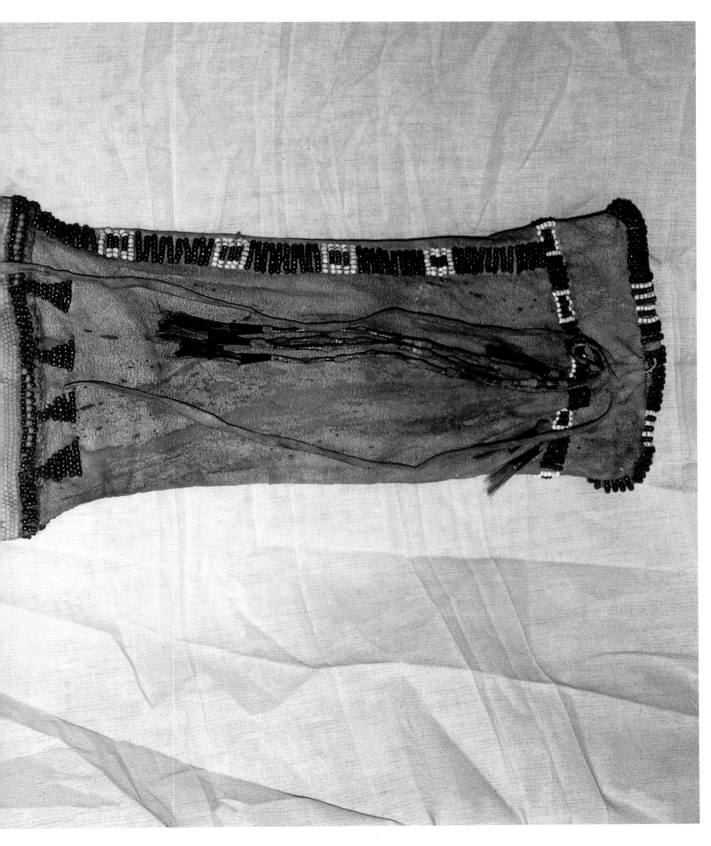

LEFT: Tobacco bag (pipe bag) c. 1840, probably Sioux. This early buckskin pipe bag has the main lower area in porcupine quillwork in a checkweave (multi-quill) technique, and quill-wrapped fringes and blue pony beadwork. It appears to be an early form of the later beaded pipe bags common in the second half of the 19th century. *Courtesy National Museums of Scotland, Edinburgh, #1937-4553*

FAR LEFT: Black Eye, Upper Yanktonai Sioux c. 1872. He holds a pipe and tobacco bag and wears a grizzly bear claw necklace.

LEFT: A typical Western (Teton) Sioux tobacco or pipe bag c. 1890. Made of buckskin and beaded in geometrical lazy-stitch, sinew-sewn designs. Buffalo Bill Historical Center, Cody, Wyoming.

RIGHT: Western (Teton) Sioux love flute in the shape of a crane's head. *Don Diessner Collection*

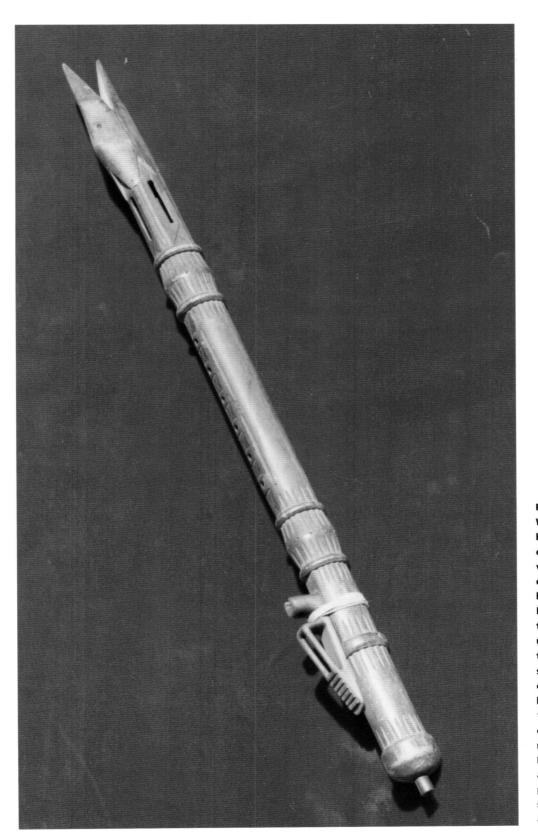

PAGES 90–91: Examples of Western (Teton) Sioux beadwork of the late 19th century. Left, a solid beaded vest or waistcoat with designs of warriors on horseback in lazy stitch or lane stitch. Right, Two tobacco bags or pipe bags, using similar beading technique with sinew. Small seed beads in a wide variety of colors (mostly Italian) became available after about 1860. The development of complex geometric designs may have been inspired by Middle Eastern rugs, alternatively a natural progression from earlier simple geometrical quillwork and beadwork designs.

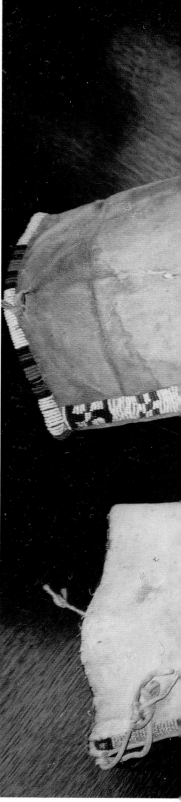

ABOVE AND ABOVE RIGHT: A pair of Teton Sioux moccasins c. 1895. They are
solidly beaded in lazy or lane-stitch technique, including the soles. These
were given as gifts or "honor" moccasins or for use when horseriding.
Incorrectly once termed "burial" moccasins. *M. G. Johnson Collection.*

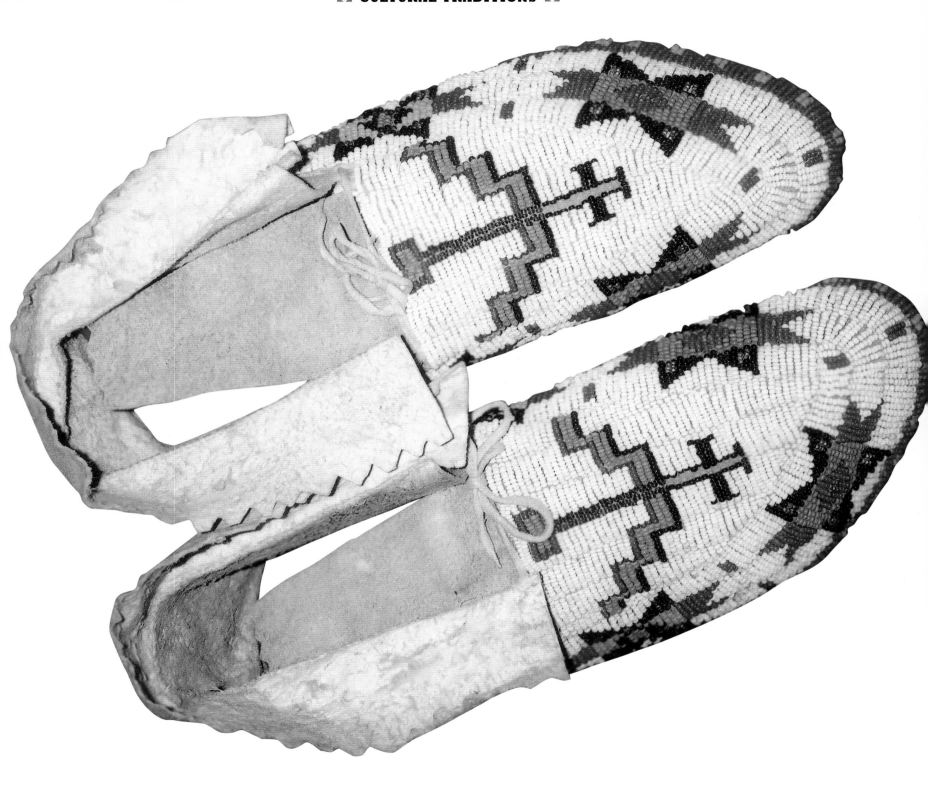

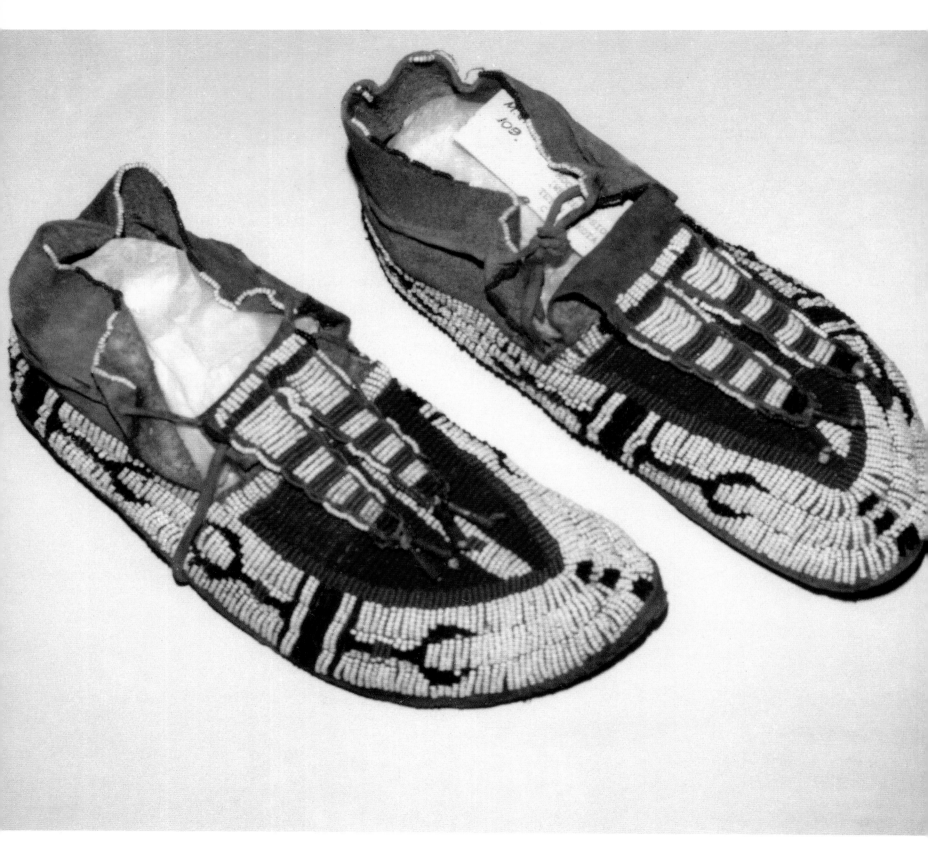

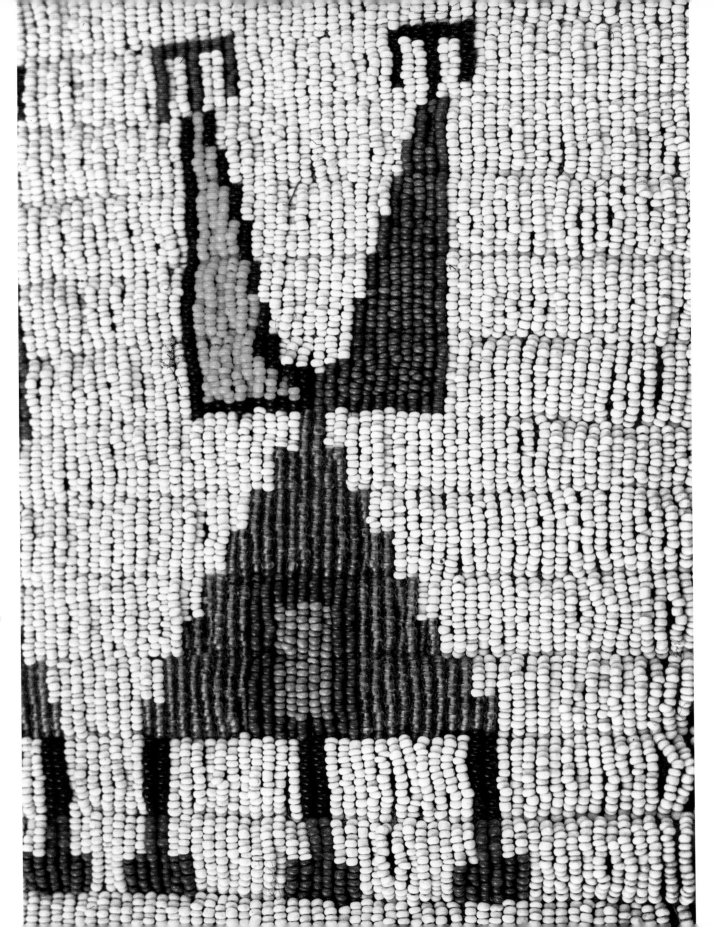

LEFT: A pair of Teton Sioux moccasins c. 1860s made of buffalo hide and fully beaded in the early, first generation of seed bead designs. Note the so-called buffalo hoof design on the instep and buffalo horns symbolically shown on the side. Formerly M. G. Johnson Collection.

RIGHT: Close up detail of lazy-stitch beadwork (or lane-stitch beadwork) c. 1880. This was the principal style of Western Sioux beadwork of the second half of the 19th century and almost entirely in geometrical designs. Much beadwork was sewn with sinew thread in stitches of 10 to 12 beads wide. The term "lazy" was adopted because it is simpler, requiring less time than two-thread appliqué work of the more northerly tribes. The seed beads were largely Venetian and available to Plains Indians from 1840 to 1890 and then replaced with Bohemian (Czechoslovakian) in more vivid colors and regular size, 0.1 to 0.3cm diameter. By comparison pony beads are 0.35 to 0.4cm in diameter.

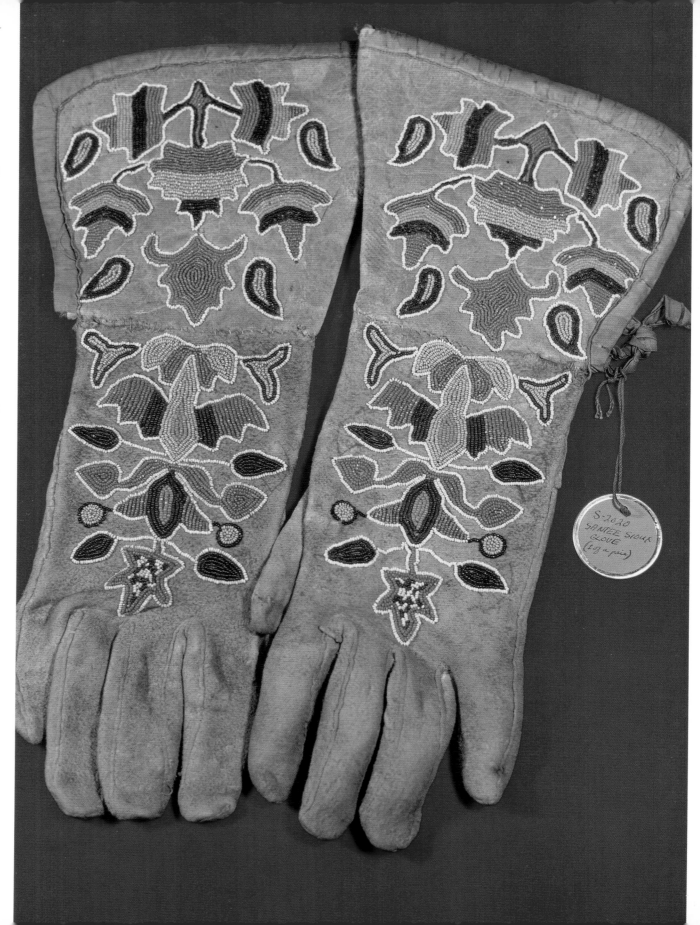

RIGHT: Gauntlet-gloves, Santee Sioux c. 1890. The buckskin gloves are decorated with one of two styles of beadwork, the Santee and their mixed bloods shared with the Canadian Métis from the Red River area of Manitoba whose inspiration for such designs probably came from French Canada and the missionaries who followed the fur trade west. *Courtesy Philbrook Art Centers, Oklahoma*

RIGHT: Beadwork on a vest, c. 1900, possibly Santee (Eastern) Sioux or Red River mixed blood. Considerable interaction took place between Red River mixed bloods and the Eastern Sioux both before and after some moved to Canada in the 1860s. The Red River mixed bloods were descendants of French and British traders and Ojibwa and Cree woman often called Métis. Their woman produced beautiful work in porcupine quills, beadwork, and silkwork, which they adorned buckskin coats, saddles, moccasins, and pouches. These mixed bloods made visits across the prairies to St. Paul to sell their produce including buffalo hides and pemmican (dried meat). Much of their artwork was semi-floral beadwork and no doubt adopted by the Santees, including the narrow leaf style shown on this vest, in lazy-stitch technique.

LEFT: Four Bears, a Chief of the Two Kettle Sioux (Teton) 1870. He holds an eagle feather fan.

RIGHT: Appliqué and woven beaded bandolier bags were usually the work of the Ojibwa Indians of Wisconsin, Minnesota, and Ontario. They were much sought after by the Santee, Yankton, and Yanktonai Sioux who would often trade horses for them. This particular example was made by a Yankton woman, Minnie Whiteshirt in the late 19th century and is indistinguishable from Ojibwa work.

FAR RIGHT: "Sioux Maiden," as published in Volume III of Edward S. Curtis' *The North American Indian.* This full-length portrait shows a young woman standing by a tree. She is wearing a beaded headband, unusual for the period—c.1907— beaded buckskin dress decorated with elks' teeth, and likely Southern Plains-made not Sioux. *Library of Congress, Prints and Photographs Collection LC-USZ62-106267*

LEFT: This is an excellent image of an early 19th century Santee Sioux bark lodge with a platform for drying corn. The woman wears center-seam moccasins, trade cloth skirt, and leggings. A Woodland style cradle holds the baby. Painting by Seth Eastman.

ABOVE: Pictographs of warriors and horses on a Plains Indian shirt, early 19th century. Note the simplistic but effective art style to portray and record a battle scene, with little or no European influence.

LEFT: Warriors and horses drawn on muslin, late 19th century. Drawings contain lifelike realistic representations of warriors' attire, weapons, hairstyles, headdresses, shields etc, in a style showing development from Euro-American influences. *Courtesy British Museum*

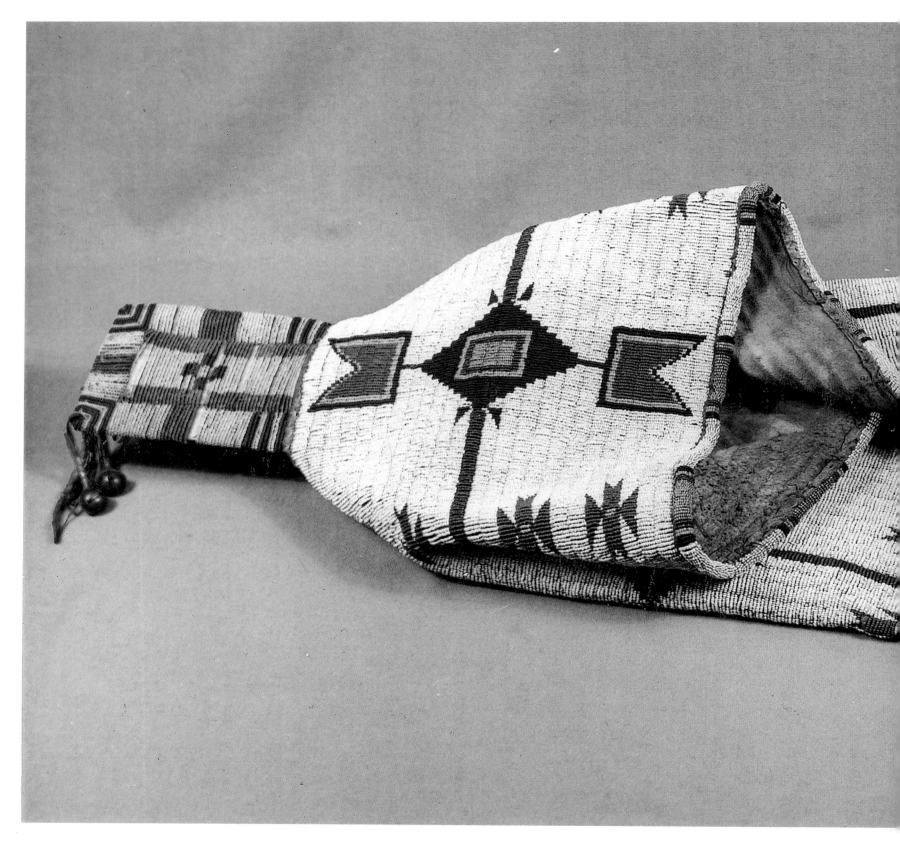

LEFT: Solid beaded Western Sioux (Teton) cradle c. 1885. Typical Western Sioux geometric designs on a white background in small seed beads of the type traded to Indians after about 1850. The ridged or arched effect is called "lazy" or "lane" stitch, and consists of eight or so beads sewn with sinew. *Pitt Rivers Museum, University of Oxford, UK*

ABOVE: Bear Foot, Western Sioux c. 1900. He holds a bow and arrows which were the primary weapons for hunting from horseback during the 19th century. Bows were made generally of ash about 3.5 feet for use on horseback and often double curved. Compound bows were made of mountain sheep or buffalo horn and both types were backed with sinew. Arrows were also often of ash about 25 inches long, fletched with three eagle feathers and grooved with lightening marks and painted. Points were bone or stone attached with glue and sinew and later made from hoop iron obtained from whites. Photographer Heyn. *Library of Congress, Prints & Photographs Division LC-USZ62-55846*

ABOVE: Western Sioux men in front of canvas tipis. Tipis were originally made of buffalo hides but after the destruction of the herds, army canvas duck was provided by the military to make tipi covers in the old pattern. Basically a tilted cone, the cover is a near half circle on plan. Covers were erected on a frame of poles (often lodge pole pine) usually by women. The "ears" shown positioned by external poles controlled the draft to remove smoke from internal fires. Canvas tipis are still seen at summer powwows. *Library of Congress, Prints & Photographs Division LC-USZ62-107545*

ABOVE: Bone Necklace, Western Sioux youth c. 1899. This young man, wearing an otter fur cape also wears a "Sacred Hoop" in his hair being a cross imposed on a circle made of rawhide and wrapped with porcupine quills. Modern Traditional Dancers are often seen with similar emblems today. Photographer Heyn. *Library of Congress, Prints & Photographs Division LC-USZ62-55848*

Religion

The Eastern branches of the Sioux had a religious society known as the Medicine Lodge which was similar to the Ojibwa "Midewiwin" (Grand Medicine Society) or Mide. The acknowledged intent of the society was to prolong human life, and to this end the lore of herbs and magical medicines was zealously guarded. Membership of the society involved a costly period of instruction by a Mide priest when candidates were initiated into four or more degrees or orders.

The society even required a price to see the final settlement of souls of the dead in their future abode. Relatives paid well for ceremonies on behalf of the deceased. Attainment of each degree of membership brought with it increased knowledge—such as the right to conduct ceremonies or to use sacred objects. One of the essential ceremonial features was the ritual "shooting" of candidates who, after falling down as if dead, were revived and spiritually renewed into a new and moral beginning. Many ceremonies were carried out in a specially constructed long, brush-covered lodge. Mide paraphernalia consisted of long records of mnemonic figures on wooden slabs which conveyed the precise details of the rituals, specially decorated animal-skin medicine bags for "doctoring" at each degree, and carved feast bowls. The Medicine Lodge religion is thought to have been a post-contact religion in response to changing cultural conditions. However it was unknown to the Western Sioux.

The Western Sioux believed that all natural phenomena could be transformed. Things that were permanently transformed were collectively Wakantanka (Great Spirit). Man was considered powerless when confronted by nature and cried out for pity when help was required. Men addressed Wakantanka as father or grandfather and those who were answered or transformed were Wakan (holy).

Wakantanka was expressed in fours, or four times four or four times seven, i.e. four seasons, four phases of the moon, four directions. The energy of the universe was controlled and subordinate to both Wakantanka and Wakansica (evil sacred). There were 16 aspects of Wakantanka in groups of four in descending importance: Sun, Sky, Earth, and Rock; Moon, Wind, Falling Stars, Thunder Being; Two-legged being, Four Winds, Whirlwind, and Buffalo; Shade, Breath, Shade-like, and Potency. There were other supernatural forces some benevolent and others malevolent: Old Man, Spider, Old Woman, and Wizard.

Those who mediated between supernatural beings and powers were considered holy (Wakan people) and were separate from those who administered herbal medicine, pejuta Wicasa (Medicine Man). Wakan people received visions to predict good hunting, outcome of war parties, found lost objects, and interpreted sacred myths and directed ceremonials.

Dream societies were formed by men who had received visions of the same animal. The Heyoka Society received visions of the Thunder Beings, and members were required to act opposite to normal,

e.g. dress heavily in summer, scantily in winter, spoke backwards or acted as clowns. The Elk dreamers imbued of power with women and other animal cults were Bear, Black-tailed deer, Wolf, Buffalo, also a Berdache cult and Double Woman cult with power to seduce men. Wakan people were different to ordinary people because of their ability to interpret sacred knowledge and to share this knowledge with the supernatural and other holy people by means of a special sacred language.

The legend of the coming of the White Buffalo Calf Woman to the Sans Arc band probably coincides with the reformation of the Teton Sioux religion which probably occurred about the time they were increasing in number and power and transforming into a truly nomadic plains people 1750–1800. The legend explains how she gave directions for a number of rites to influence the supernatural beings to a band of Sans Arc under Standing Buffalo after meeting two of his scouts looking for buffalo. She presented a sacred calf pipe bundle to them directing them in its use in rituals. This bundle, or a form of it, is said to still exist on the Cheyenne River Reservation, South Dakota to this day. She gave instructions for the seven rituals as follows:

1. The Adoption rite or the Making of Relatives— Hunkalowanpi or simply Hunka.
   Its purpose was to establish closer relationships between men and to bond them together ceremonially involving the use of special wands decorated with feathers and horsetails.

2. The Sun Dance—Wiwayankwacipi.
   A calendrial world renewal ceremony usually held in early summer when several bands came together for a common buffalo hunt. The rite was

LEFT: Hunka ritual, see page 108. Here Slow Bull, Saliva, and Picket Pin prepare for the ceremony, c. 1908. Published in *The North American Indian* by Edward S. Curtis, Seattle, Washington, Volume III. *Library of Congress, Prints & Photographs Division, Edward S. Curtis Collection, LC-USZ62-112247*

undertaken to fulfil the vows of men or women by praying for tribal well-being and return of the buffalo. The ceremony was performed in a large lodge of posts and rafters covered with brush. The rafters adjoin a supporting center pole which had been "captured" by warriors, erected vertically around which the medicine lodge was constructed usually about 20 yards in diameter.

3. Vision Quest—Hanbleceyapi.
   Usually performed during adolescence to seek a vision or gain power. In order that the power never leaves the recipient he will always carry some material representing the dreamed animal or object with him.

4. Spirit-Keepers or Ghost Keeping—Wakicagapi.
   The spirit of a deceased was kept ritually before traveling south to the Milky Way,

BELOW: Hunka ritual altar.

ALTAR

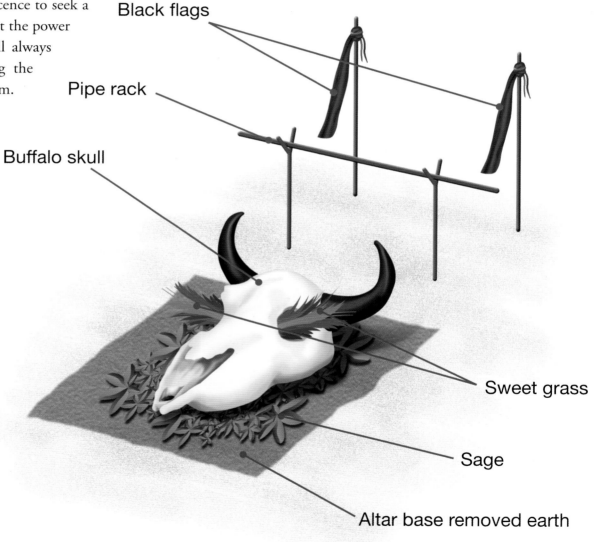

Black flags

Pipe rack

Buffalo skull

Sweet grass

Sage

Altar base removed earth

ABOVE: Sun Dancing at Pine Ridge Reservation, South Dakota. Oglala (Teton) Sioux c. 1960. The Sun Dance was the most important of all Plains Indian ceremonies. It was a world renewal or re-creation ceremony and formerly held in June to ensure the return each year of the buffalo, although recent modified nativistic versions of the rite are often celebrated in July or August. See caption on page 115.

sometimes up to two years before the soul was released.

5. Throwing of the Ball—Tapawankayeyapi.
Based upon the legend of a buffalo calf who grew into a woman who had a ball made which symbolically represented the universe which was used in ritual games.

6. Girl's Puberty Ritual also known as the Buffalo Rite—Atankalowanpi.
Established a pubescent girl's relationship to the sacred White Buffalo Calf Woman.

7. The Sweat Lodge, the Rite of Purification—Initipi.
Communal purification in a heated sweat lodge, a small circular dome-shaped lodge with hot stones.

One of the principal religious symbols of the Sioux is the hoop or circle that illustrates the completeness of all things in nature. Another important Sioux symbol is the Greek (equal-armed) Cross. This symbolizes the four winds or directions, the corners of the universe. Each point of the cross has its own color symbol: white for north, red for east, yellow for south, and black (or blue) for west.

LEFT AND RIGHT: The basic pattern of the Sun Dance ritual was highly uniform and initiated in the winter months by a man or woman who had vowed to do so or had visionary command to do so. The ritual was held in a "lodge" of 10 to 20 posts up to 20 yards in diameter, with an entrance to the east, covered with brush with rafters attached to a center pole, which had been ritually prepared beforehand. The center pole had a bundle of brush near the top representing the thunderbird's nest, also attached would be a head or skin of a buffalo bull and offerings of other objects such as a doll or cloth would be affixed. The public performance of the ceremonial began with formal procession of barefooted, kilt-clad, painted dancers into the lodge, gazing constantly at the center-pole, bending their knees, blowing their eagle-bone whistles to arouse the pity of a supernatural being. Other ceremonies were held concerning curing the sick, exhibitions of supernatural power, distribution of wealth and finally some dancers who had vowed to do so would be pierced through the pectoral muscles by skewers and attached to the center pole. Dancing back and forth attempting to tear themselves free gaining supernatural power through their ecstasy of pain. Banned for many years by the U.S. Government officials, shortened versions are held today on most Sioux reservations.

SUN DANCE LODGE

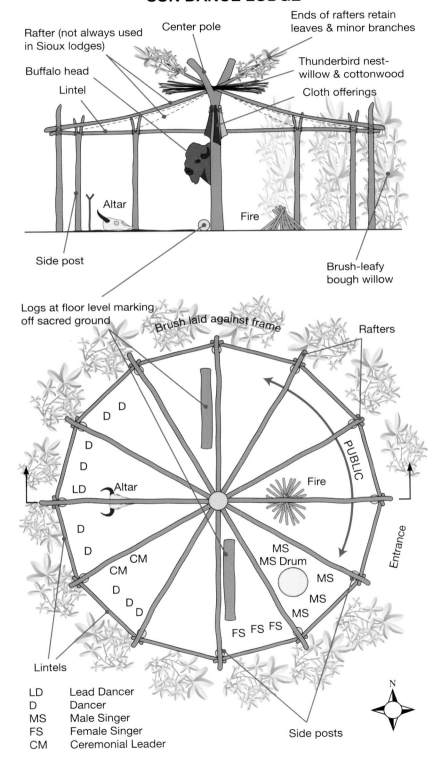

Rafter (not always used in Sioux lodges)

Buffalo head

Lintel

Center pole

Ends of rafters retain leaves & minor branches

Thunderbird nest-willow & cottonwood

Cloth offerings

Altar

Fire

Side post

Brush-leafy bough willow

Logs at floor level marking off sacred ground

Brush laid against frame

Rafters

PUBLIC

D
D
D
D
LD   Altar
D
D
D
CM
CM
D
D D
FS FS FS

Fire

MS
MS Drum
MS
MS
MS

Entrance

Lintels

Side posts

N

LD   Lead Dancer
D   Dancer
MS   Male Singer
FS   Female Singer
CM   Ceremonial Leader

The arms east to west indicate the path of good; south to north the path of war or calamity. The cross when superimposed on the circle produces the "sacred hoop" or medicine wheel. Small versions cut from rawhide and wrapped with quills are often worn as hair ornaments by traditional dancers. The Thunderbird—thought of as a giant eagle—was the chief of powers above the earth with its flapping wings (thunder) and flashing eyes (lightning), but as it brought rain was generally considered benevolent. Individuals who dreamed of the Thunderbird had to join the Heyoka cult or Society of Clowns, who moved in a strange backward manner and were regarded with a mixture of horror and fear. They appeared in this fashion at least once a year dressed in ragged costume and masks. To dream of Double Woman was to have a vision conferring unusual skill. Among the Santees a Double Woman dreamer claimed to have been taught to make sashes, kneebands, and turbans, and all became good craftworkers. The "Little Tree Dweller" was generally considered malevolent and caused hunters to lose their way or spoiled their luck. Of all the animals the Sioux believed to possess and to be able to confer medicine power, the grizzly bear ranked first.

LEFT: Teton Sioux Sun Dance, probably Oglalas c. 1930. Note the fully beaded yokes on the buckskin dresses worn by two women. *O'Neill Photo Co.*

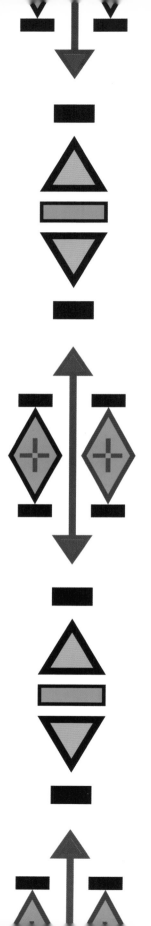

Recent Sioux History and Panindianism

During the early 20th century reservation populations evolved into a number of social groups divided by economics, religion, social achievement, and blood quantum. As a range (cattle) economy was the only viable one on the large reservations, unemployment became endemic as Indian communities were geographically isolated. In 1928 the Meriam Report called attention to the Indian conditions and set the stage for a change of government policy. In 1934 the Wheeler-Howard Act (Indian Reorganization Act) was passed, giving Indians some control of tribal affairs and the bureaucracies of the Bureau of Indian Affairs (BIA), a branch of the Department of the Interior. The most important change was in education. However, the result was that it pushed further the modernization of the mixed bloods and precipitated their entrance into the larger society, often off reservations. World War II opened up further off-reservation employment opportunities for the Sioux, and by mixing with Indians from other tribal groups in towns and cities there grew a gradual inter-tribal identity which anthropologists have termed "Panindianism." The American Indian Movement (AIM) initially founded in cities by acculturated college-educated Métis successfully brought to the attention of the American public wrongs perpetrated against the Native American, and in particular the corruption of the mixed-blood controlled tribal councils such as those at Pine Ridge in the 1970s where a stand-off between AIM and government officials became a symbolic statement of continued federal injustices to all American Indians.

However, the most obvious manifestation of panindianism has been the nationwide development of the ubiquitous "Powwow" and it is from among the Sioux that we find some of the historic roots of modern panindianism, which is in some degree an extension of the old plains culture. The old Sioux wacipi is now the powwow and they received the old original Grass Dance from the Omaha sometime in the 1860s. It was, for the Omahas and Pawnee, a war society dance, but to the Sioux it became largely social and as such acceptable to government officials for July 4 celebrations. With the Grass or Omaha Dance (wrongly also called War Dance) the Sioux had—and continued to celebrate—some vestige of traditional culture, dance dress, and traditional songs. Today the "contemporary traditional" male dancer is a direct result of this tradition. However the Sioux have absorbed panindian influences from other areas, most notably from about 1920 on from Oklahoma—two forms of Oklahoma war dances, grand entries, round dances, stomp dances, and contests. From the Northern Plains, two revised forms of Grass Dances arrived during the 1960s and 1980s, with many new powwow songs.

The Sioux have also continued to hold Sun Dances, if somewhat shortened versions. The tribal council at Pine Ridge attempted to commercialize the event in the 1960s. Also held are vision quests, sweat lodges, memorial feasts, wakes, and night cult

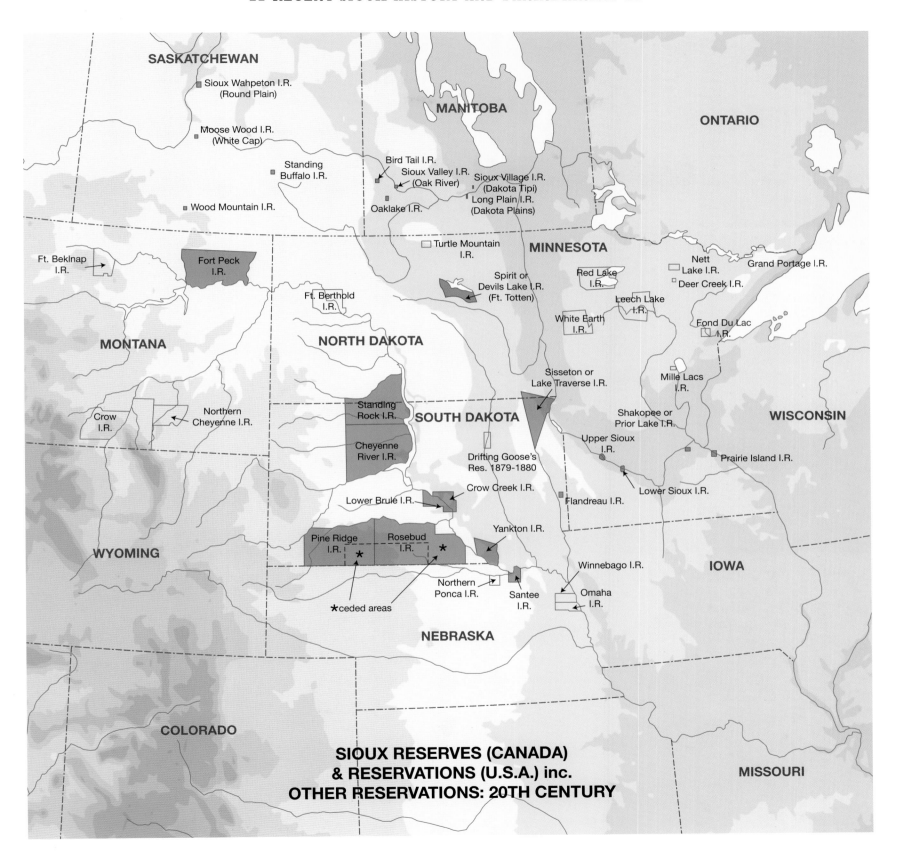

SASKATCHEWAN

Sioux Wahpeton I.R.
(Round Plain)

Moose Wood I.R.
(White Cap)

Standing
Buffalo I.R.

Wood Mountain I.R.

MANITOBA

Bird Tail I.R.
Sioux Valley I.R.
(Oak River)

Sioux Village I.R.
(Dakota Tipi)
Long Plain I.R.
(Dakota Plains)

Oaklake I.R.

ONTARIO

Ft. Beklnap
I.R.

Fort Peck
I.R.

MONTANA

Crow
I.R.

Northern
Cheyenne I.R.

Ft. Berthold
I.R.

NORTH DAKOTA

Turtle Mountain
I.R.

MINNESOTA

Spirit or
Devils Lake I.R.
(Ft. Totten)

Red Lake
I.R.

White Earth
I.R.

Nett
Lake I.R.

Grand Portage I.R.

Deer Creek I.R.

Leech Lake
I.R.

Fond Du Lac
I.R.

Sisseton or
Lake Traverse I.R.

Mille Lacs
I.R.

WISCONSIN

Standing
Rock I.R.

SOUTH DAKOTA

Shakopee or
Prior Lake I.R.

Upper Sioux
I.R.

Prairie Island I.R.

Cheyenne
River I.R.

Drifting Goose's
Res. 1879-1880

Crow Creek I.R.

Lower Brule I.R.

Lower Sioux I.R.

Flandreau I.R.

Yankton I.R.

Pine Ridge
I.R.

Rosebud
I.R.

✶

✶

Winnebago I.R.

IOWA

WYOMING

✶ceded areas

Northern
Ponca I.R.

Santee
I.R.

Omaha
I.R.

NEBRASKA

COLORADO

**SIOUX RESERVES (CANADA)
& RESERVATIONS (U.S.A.) inc.
OTHER RESERVATIONS: 20TH CENTURY**

MISSOURI

RIGHT: Shot In The Eye, half-length portrait, facing front, wearing warbonnet, holding a pipe. Adolph Muhr photographer c. 1899 but published by Rinehart of Omaha. *Library of Congress, Prints & Photographs Division LC-USZC2-6293*

rituals (Yuwipis). Another most important and common ceremony held at Sioux community dances is the adoption or "Hunka" ceremony, sometimes called the Plume ceremony today. There are also ceremonies honoring graduates, veterans, and Powwow committee members. Powwows are held in all Sioux reservations, and where casinos have enhanced the local economy, huge cash prizes are offered for the best male and female dancers and costumes in various categories. A revival of, and interest in, craftwork augments the powwow scene. However, the regular use of native language by the younger generations is rapidly decreasing and they will probably not survive as a first language long into the 21st century. Unfortunately, problems with alcohol and drugs still abound causing family breakdown. Average family incomes are still far below national levels. The Sioux remain very patriotic, having men who served with distinction in all the major American conflicts of the 20th and 21st centuries. The Native American Church (Peyote), a part-Indian and part-Christian religion, also continues to have strong membership on several reservations.

At Sioux dances and powwows in South and North Dakota women can be observed performing several distinctly different styles of dancing and wearing appropriate dress for each. The most conservative dancing is the "old time" ladies style when they stand around the outside of the dance arena and bob in place or move slightly clockwise. They flex their knees and ankles and use their arms to emphasize their bounce to the music. Many of these ladies wear traditional skin or woolen dresses and may also carry a shawl or blanket around their waist. The second style, a more recent and popular style of ladies dance, began some time after World War II. Sioux women began to dance in a line

outside the circle of dancing men at social dances and powwows using a "flat step" that probably derived from Oklahoma Indians. They are usually dressed simply with a shawl or blanket, perhaps moccasins together with an elegant non-Indian skirt and blouse. The third style are young ladies or teenage girls who dress with heavily fringed shawls and dance in all parts of the dance arena. They dance in fancy skipping steps and with intricate footwork. These "Shawl Dancers" are demonstrating an innovative style of women's dance that seems to have begun in the 1970s. More recently Sioux girls have adopted the "jingle dress" costume, a basic cloth dress covered with tin-cone jingles which gives a distinctive sound as the dancers move. Some girls will dance together in unison thus emphasizing the sound. For a time in the mid-1960s some girls began to adopt men's dance clothes and dance styles but this is not often seen today. Women also dance in the rabbit dances (round dances and two-steps) held mostly by request at indoor dances, and some women still retain and exercise their privilege of choosing their partners.

The traditional men's style dancing was, and still is, the "Grass" or "Omaha" style, which characteristic features are the concentrated use of head and shoulders, facial expressions, and footwork in time with singing. Some influences from Oklahoma panindian dancing and costume disseminated to the Sioux during the period 1930–50 with emphasis on fancy footwork, abrupt changes in posture, and spins and a newer northern Grass Dance style arrived on the Sioux reservations in the 1950s with dancers shaking shoulders and swaying torsos, a style which apparently came from Canada. However the Sioux themselves have made a major contribution to panindianism by their development of the so-called "contemporary traditional" man's dance costume

LEFT: Mr. and Mrs. Iron Nest, Brulé (Teton) Sioux c. 1900. Note the mature eagle feather bonnet and beaded shirt. Mrs. Iron Nest wears a cloth dress with elk teeth decoration. The log cabin in the background gives some idea of the dreadful conditions the Sioux people endured during the early reservation years, and which still continue today in some areas. Photograph F. C. Cundill, Trail City, South Dakota.

FAR LEFT: Sunflower, Western (Teton) Sioux man c. 1899. He wears a beaded vest with typical geometrical designs, hairpipe breastplate, and otter fur cape. Photographer Herman Heyn. *Library of Congress, Prints & Photographs Division* LC-USZ62-101211

which became popular during the last quarter of the 20th century and spread to Indians throughout the United States and Canada. Yet another Grass Dance costume became popular in the 1980s with emphasis on heavy woolen fringing. The traditional dance costume consisted of a porcupine and deer-tail headdress, beaded moccasins, cuffs, arm bands, bone chokers, hairpipe breastplates, and sequined aprons on basic dyed long underwear or shirts and trousers of non-Indian make. Bustles were clusters of predatory-bird feathers called mess bustles or the symbolic "Crow Bustle" a back bustle constructed of feathers from birds which scavenged battlefields. At the beginning of the 20th century many older men still wore warbonnets, buckskin shirts, and leggings, but by the 1960s this style of dress and old dance

costumes had been replaced by poorly simulated Oklahoma fancy dance costume, and the northern grass dance outfits replete with heavy matching beadwork, fringes, wide belts, and larger cuffs. The modern contemporary traditional style, which has made a huge impact since the 1980s, consists of a porcupine hair roach, hairpipe breastplate, matching beaded bands, arm cuffs, and knee bands, large aprons, moccasins, sometimes a beaded vest, and belt with side drops. The back bustle is now a large wheel of matched eagle feathers with cloth trailers. Face painting is also a distinctive feature of the costume. Although this style incorporates dress elements from the original Grass or Omaha society style of the 19th century the modern Grass Dance with its woolen fringing is quite separate. The origin of the name "Grass Dance" refers to the bunches of sweet grass tucked into the belt to represent scalps in the old regalia's symbolism.

Population of the Sioux at the beginning of the 21st century

The figures shown are enrolled or registered members. Fewer than half live on the reserves and many have only small amounts of Indian ancestry. There are large Sioux populations in cities such as Denver. Perhaps less than 20 percent of these official figures are near or full blood Indian people. Some Sioux groups today use their reservation names as tribal names e.g. Cheyenne River Sioux, Rosebud Sioux, and Pine Ridge Sioux (or Oglala Sioux). Many Western Sioux prefer to be called "Lakota," their name in their own language.

RIGHT: Mato Wammyomai and Mato Pahin. Two Western Sioux Grass Dancers c. 1898. The old Grass or Omaha Dance came to the Teton (Western) Sioux about 1860–70 from the Omaha tribe bringing a number of old warrior society features of the Missouri River valley tribes. Most prominent was the so-called "Crow Bustle" a collection of feathers worn on the back constructed from feathers of birds who scavenged a battlefield, the Crow being the first. The two upright feathers represent fallen warriors, one a friend the other an enemy. The ensemble was held around the waist sometimes with a sash in which braids of sweetgrass representing scalps were held—hence the term "Grass Dance." Both dancers are wearing such bustles. Photographer Heyn. *Library of Congress, Prints & Photographs Division LC-USZ62-54488*

Country, Province or State	Reserve (Canada) or Reservation (US)	Division	Enrolled population 2001 (US) 2005 (Canada)
CANADA			
Manitoba	Sioux Village (Dakota tipi)	Wahpeton	280
"	Long Plain (Dakota Plains)	Wahpeton and Sisseton	237
"	Sioux Valley (Oak River)	Sisseton, Mdewakanton Wahpekute, Wahpeton	2,176
"	Birdtail	Mdewakanton, Wahpeton Yanktonai	686
"	Oak Lake (pipestone)	Wahpekute, Wahpeton Yanktonai	572
Saskatchewan	Standing Buffalo (Fort Qu'Appelle)	Sisseton, Wahpeton	1,078
"	Moose Woods (White Caps)	Sisseton	474
"	Sioux Wahpeton (Round Plain)	Wahpeton	439
"	Wood Mountain	Hunkpapa	214
UNITED STATES			
Montana	Fort Peck	Lower Yanktonai, Sisseton Wahpekute, Wahpeton	11,248 With Assinibaine
North Dakota	Devil's Lake (Spirit Lake)	Wahpeton, Sisseton Upper Yanktonai	4,948
North & South Dakota	Standing Rock	Upper Yanktonai	7,380 (N. Dakota)
		Hunkpapa, Blackfeet Sans Arc, Two Kettle	6,039 (S. Dakota)
South Dakota	Lake Traverse	Sisseton, Wahpeton	10,759
"	Flandreau	Wahpeton	716
"	Cheyenne River	Minneconjon, Blackfeet Two Kettle, Sans Arc	13,507
"	Crow Creek	Lower Yanktonai	3,507
"	Lower Brulé	Brulé	2,627
"	Yankton	Yankton	7,570
"	Pine Ridge	Oglala, few Brulé	41,226
"	Rosebud	Brulé, few Oglala	24,134
Minnesota	Upper Sioux	Mdewakanton, Sisseton Wahpeton	404
"	Lower Sioux	Mdewakanton Wahpekute	820
"	Prior Lake (Shakopee)	Mdewakanton Wahpekute	326
"	Prairie Island	Mdewakanton Wahpekute	622
Nebraska	Santee	Mdewakanton Wahpekute	2,663
		TOTAL	144,415

LEFT: Two Western Sioux women cutting meat and drying it on racks to prepare jerky (thinly sliced beef dried in the sun) or pemmican (dried meat pounded with berries and fat), c. 1908. Published in *The North American Indian* by Edward S. Curtis. *Library of Congress, Prints & Photographs Division, Edward S. Curtis Collection, LC-USZ62-101184*

LEFT: Pine Ridge Sioux Indians drying meat into jerky (thinly sliced beef dried in the sun) and pemmican (dried meat pounded with berries and fat). Photograph made by S. D. Butcher & Son, Kearney, Nebraska, c. 1908. *Library of Congress, Prints & Photographs Division LC-DIG-ppmsca-08384*

RIGHT: Mr. Williams or Azizi (Whispering), Eastern (Santee) Sioux, Ft. Totten, North Dakota, c. 1930. Note the pipe and tobacco bag. Photograph Louis Garcia.

ABOVE: Little Wound and nine other Western Sioux chiefs wearing eagle feather headdresses and traditional attire. Feather symbolism had developed to a high degree among the Sioux in the early 19th century; however, during the reservation period bonnets had lost their significance and men wore eagle feather headdresses who were not previously entitled to do so, c. 1899. Photo by Heyn. *Library of Congress, Prints & Photographs DivisionLC-USZ62-101268*

RIGHT: High Bear, Brulé (Western) Sioux man cooking by throwing heated stones into a buffalo or cattle-stomach pouch filled with water, Rosebud Indian Reservation, c. 1911. *Library of Congress, Prints & Photographs Division LC-USZ62-101274*

PRIMITIVE COOKING.

COPYRIGHT 1911 BY J. A. ANDERSON.

RIGHT: Crow Dog, Brulé (Western) Sioux, c. 1900, holding a Remington bolt-action rifle similar to those issued by the U.S. Government to the Indian police. Crow Dog was reported to have been the killer of Spotted Tail near the Rosebud Agency on August 5, 1881. Crow Dog believed his life was in peril and shot in self-defense during a dispute. J. A. Anderson photograph. *Library of Congress, Prints & Photographs Division LC-USZ62-102187*

LEFT: Walter Iron Shell, Brulé (Western) Sioux, probably a grandson of the old chief Iron Shell. Note the buffalo in the beaded armband, and his face painting. Although the photograph is dated 1911, it is likely a Rinehart, c. 1898. *Library of Congress, Prints & Photographs Division LC-USZ62-104565*

RIGHT: Oglala (Western) Sioux women dancing (back view) at Pine Ridge Reservation c. 1908. Note the German silver hair-plates worn on their belts, and trade cloth dresses. A number of women are wearing war bonnets perhaps in honor of their husbands. Photograph S. D. Butcher and Son. *Library of Congress, Prints & Photographs Division LC-DIG-ppmsca-08387*

BELOW RIGHT: Oglala (Western) Sioux women dancing at Pine Ridge Reservation c. 1908. Many women are wearing feather war bonnets. The standing man in ordinary white man's clothes is the celebrated Chief American Horse. Photograph S. D. Butcher and Son. *Library of Congress, Prints & Photographs Division LC-DIG-ppmsca-08386*

LEFT: Mr. and Mrs. Claude Irish and Dora Irish, Eastern (Santee) Sioux, Ft. Totten, North Dakota, c. 1930. Note the bone "hairpipes" strung horizontally for the man and vertically for the woman. These were commercially made in New Jersey and elsewhere, and sold to Indians after 1870. The woman wears dentalium shell earrings also obtained from traders. Photograph Dennis Cavanaugh and Louis Garcia.

RIGHT: Paul Iron Rope, Oglala (Teton) Sioux c. 1930. He wears the typical male dancers' dress for social dances, particularly for the Grass Dance or Omaha Dance, of the first half of the 20th century. He wears a porcupine and deer hair roach, beaded headband, armbands, and cuffs, also a neck bustle.

LEFT: Sitting Bull, Hunkpapa (Teton) Sioux, and William F. Cody (Buffalo Bill). Sitting Bull made one tour with Cody's Wild West Show. Note he wears an Ojibwa bandolier bag and Crow shirt. The eagle feather trailer bonnet is likely Sioux made. Photograph David Notman 1885.

LEFT: Laura Standing Bear and Luther Standing Bear jr. with Buffalo Bill's Wild West Show 1902–03. She wears a woolen tradecloth dress decorated with dentalium shells.

RIGHT: Red Horn Bull, a Western Sioux Indian from Buffalo Bill's Wild West Show holding a stone-headed club, c. 1900. *Library of Congress, Prints & Photographs Division LC-DIG-ppmsca-12088*

LEFT: Shooting Pieces, a Western Sioux Indian from Buffalo Bill's Wild West Show with beaded blanket strip and holding a stone-headed club; c. 1900. *Library of Congress, Prints & Photographs Division LC-DIG-ppmsca-12104*

ABOVE LEFT and ABOVE: Painted Horse, Oglala (Teton) Sioux. Photographed at Earls Court, London c. 1909. Considerable numbers of Sioux men and women obtained employment in various touring Wild West shows such as William Cody's (Buffalo Bill's Wild West) between 1880 and 1920s. Painted Horse wears an eagle wing feather headdress, buckskin shirt, leggings, and holds a tobacco bag. Note, the same shirt was once on display at the Buffalo Bill Historical Center, Cody, Wyoming, but now seems lost, as recent searches have failed to produce the superb specimen.

LEFT: Charging Thunder, a Western Sioux Indian from Buffalo Bill's Wild West Show with porcupine quilled armband, c. 1900. For many seasons Colonel William F. Cody (Buffalo Bill and other showmen) hired Indians from the Sioux reservations to tour the American eastern states and Europe (including Great Britain on three occasions 1887, 1891, and 1903–05). They thrilled audiences with mock battles and "war dances." *Library of Congress, Prints & Photographs Division LC-DIG-ppmsca-12107*

LEFT: Chief Hollow Horn Bear, Brulé (Western Sioux) 1898. He was one of the seven sons of old Chief Iron Shell. A warrior at Little Bighorn he later became a tribal diplomat to Washington D.C. on several occasions. His likeness was used on a 14 cent United States postage stamp of 1923. This photograph is one of many taken during the Trans-Mississippi Exposition in Omaha of Indians who attended, and published by Rinehart although the actual photographer was often Adolph Muhr. *Library of Congress, Prints & Photographs Division LC-U.S.Z62-135360*

LEFT: Chief Buffalo Bear and his wife 1921. Although unfortunately damaged, this photograph shows the magnificence of Sioux dress. *Library of Congress, Prints & Photographs Division LC-DIG-npcc-04495*

ABOVE: White Calf and Iron Crow, Western Sioux c. 1925. Both men have typical Sioux eagle feather bonnets worn sloping backwards, showing the trade cloth wrapping at the base of each feather where they are attached to the skullcap just above the beaded brow band. White Calf wears a beaded vest with a horse design and Iron Crow wears a buckskin shirt with beaded strips and ermine skins, he also holds a pipe tomahawk, eagle feather fan, and pipe bag. *Library of Congress, Prints & Photographs Division LC-DIG-npcc-13464*

FAR LEFT: Contemporary traditional male dancer wearing roach, back bustle, otter fur breast piece. A Pan-Teton (Pan-Lakota) contribution to men's Panindian dance outfit styles of the late 20th century.

LEFT: Woman's traditional costume. She wears a solid beaded cape or yoke over her buckskin dress, with long fringing. She holds an eagle feather fan. This style of dress descends directly from Western Sioux dresses of the late 19th century. United Tribes Powwow Bismarck, North Dakota, Sept 1988. Photograph Jonathan Smith.

RIGHT: Woman's Fancy Shawl Dance costume. The large wrap around shawl is decorated with ribbonwork. Photograph Jonathan Smith.

FAR RIGHT: Northern Grass Dance male dancer. The outfit consists of a roach, two beaded suspenders, and much woolen fringing. This style was adopted by some Sioux dancers from North Dakota and Canadian Indians from the 1950s to the 1980s. United Tribes Powwow Bismarck, North Dakota, Sept 1988. Photograph Jonathan Smith.

Chiefs and Warriors

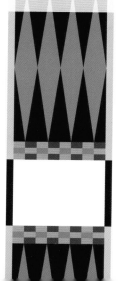

Crazy Horse

Oglala (Teton) Sioux. Born near Bear Butte, South Dakota about 1840, he was present at several fights at an early age. He led the decoys in the Fetterman battle and was also at the Wagon-Box Fight. When the Sioux went on the warpath in 1875 on account of the occupancy of the Black Hills, he fought General Crook and confronted him again on June 17, 1876, and decisively halted his advance. Joining Gall and Sitting Bull at the Little Bighorn he helped annihilate Custer's column. However, his camp was destroyed by Col. Mackenzie's 4th Cavalry near the Tongue River the following winter. He was placed under arrest and was stabbed and killed while allegedly trying to escape from Camp Robinson, Nebraska in September 1877.

Gall (Pizi)

A chief of the Hunkpapa (Teton) Sioux, born on the Grand River, South Dakota in 1840, he died at Oak Creek, South Dakota in December 1894. One of the principal chiefs at the Battle of the Little Bighorn of June 1876, he was a lieutenant of Sitting Bull but with much greater military qualities. He fled to Canada after the Custer battle but surrendered to the U.S. military on January 1, 1881, and settled on the Standing Rock Reservation. He later denounced Sitting Bull as a fraud, and befriended the whites becoming a judge of the Court for Indian Offences. He agreed to the break up of the Great Sioux Reservation of 1889.

He Dog (Sunka Bloka)
Oglala (Teton) Sioux. Born about 1840, he gained a reputation as a warrior in the 1860s. A member of the Crow Owner warrior society and a "shirt wearer." Took part in the Battle of the Little Bighorn but surrendered at Ft. Robinson in May 1877. He lived at the Cut Meat District of the Rosebud Reservation and died in 1936.

Hollow Horn Bear (Mato He Oblogeca)
Brulé (Teton) Sioux. The son of Iron Shell, he was a young warrior at the Little Bighorn. It was said he survived as a child the Battle of Bluewater in Nebraska when found by soldiers. After his surrender in 1876 he became known as a progressive leader who advanced the adoption of the white man's way of life.

Inkpaduta (Red-on-Top)
Wahpekute (Santee) Sioux. Chief of a band of Wahpekute who were openly hostile to white settlers from the early 1850s on, he led an attack on the white settlers at Spirit Lake on the Iowa-Minnesota border in 1857. Later his band joined the Western Sioux, being the only Eastern Sioux at the Battle of the Little Bighorn in 1876.

John Otherday (Angpetu-tokecha)
Wahpeton Sioux. Son of Red Bird and chief of the Wahpetons at Lac qui Parle, Minnesota, as a young man he was "passionate and revengeful" but devoted to his tribesman, saving the life of at least two kinsmen in fights with the Chippewa. He adopted the ways of the white man and became a devoted member of Dr. Williamson's church. Saved the lives of whites during Inkpaduta (1857) and Minnesota (1862) outbreaks. He was employed by Gen. Sibley as a scout and participated in the battles of Birch

Coolie and Wood Lake. Congress granted him $2,500 for his services. His final years were at Sisseton Reservation, South Dakota where he died in 1871.

Joseph White Bull (Pte-san-hunka)
Minneconjou (Teton) Sioux. One of the foremost warriors during the late 1860s and 1870s, he was the son of Makes Room and nephew of Sitting Bull. He was in the Fetterman fight in 1866 near Ft. Phil Kearney. He was a warrior at the Little Bighorn and was later advanced by Stanley Vestal, the historian, as the warrior who killed George A. Custer in personal combat.

Luther Standing Bear
Brulé (Teton) Sioux 1863–1936. Author of *My People the Sioux* and several other books on Indian life, he has no connection with the Minneconjou of the same name. He, his wife, and son toured Great Britain with Buffalo Bill's Wild West Show in 1902–03.

Rain-in-the-Face
Hunkpapa (Teton) Sioux. Born about 1835, he died at Standing Rock Reservation in September 1905. He apparently obtained his name after a fight with a Cheyenne receiving several blows causing his face to be spattered with blood. The name was similarly reinforced after a fight with Gros Ventres in the rain. He was as a warrior in the war party which killed Capt. Fetterman and 90 soldiers near Ft. Phil Kearney, Wyoming in December 1866, and fought at Ft. Totten in 1868. He was a leading participant in the Little Bighorn fight where he was wounded. He fled to Canada where he remained until 1880 and later surrendered to General Miles at Ft. Keogh, Montana.

FAR LEFT: Luther Standing Bear, Brulé (Teton) Sioux, pictures on a postcard for the British tour of Buffalo Bill's Wild West Show 1902–03. He wears a trailer eagle feather bonnet and typical Sioux regalia of the early 20th century. Standing Bear became a successful author.

LEFT: Rain-in-the-Face (Iromagaja). *The Art Archive/National Archives Washington D.C.*

Red Cloud (Murpiya Luta)

Oglala (Teton) Sioux. Born about 1822 near the forks of the Platte River, he became the principal War Chief on the Bozeman Trail with attacks on the protecting forts (C. F. Smith, Phil Kearney, and Reno) during the 1860s. Chief of the hostiles who destroyed Capt. Fetterman's detachment in 1866, he later lost many warriors at the Wagon-Box Fight. He signed the 1868 Laramie Treaty and burned the abandoned forts. He subsequently lived on the Pine Ridge Reservation. He took no part in the Sioux war of 1876. He died in December 1909.

Red Thunder

Yanktonai Sioux, also known as Shappa or Beaver. He met Lt. Z. M. Pike at the great council at Prairie du Chien, Wisconsin in 1806 who pronounced him the most gorgeously dressed chief attending. He fought with his son Wanata with the British in the War of 1812 at Ft. Meigs and at Sandusky, Ohio. He was killed by Chippewa in 1823.

Sleepy Eyes (Ishtaba)

A Sisseton (Santee) Sioux Chief born near the site of Mankota, Minnesota, he lived most of his life in Brown Country, Minnesota. He was prominent in the affairs of the Eastern Sioux before the uprising of 1862–63 and signed most of the major treaties with the U.S. between 1825 and 1851.

Sitting Bull (Tatanka Yotanka)

Born a Hunkpapa (Teton) Sioux on the Grand River South Dakota in 1834. He gained influence being a skilful peacemaker and medicine man. He took an active part in the Indian wars of the 1860s including the raid on Ft. Buford. He predicted the defeat of Custer during a Sun Dance held prior to the battle. Although he does not seem to have taken an active

LEFT: Red Cloud (Murpiya Luta or Mahpina). The shirt he is wearing is now in the Buffalo Bill Historical Center, Cody, Wyoming. *The Art Archive/National Archives Washington D.C.*

FAR LEFT: Esh-Ta-Leah or Ishtaba also called "Sleepy Eyes" a Sisseton (Santee) Sioux Chief who signed the treaties of Prairie du Chien 1825 and St. Peters of 1836. His band lived below Lake Traverse, Minnesota. He and his son signed the Traverse des Sioux Treaty of 1851. From a lithograph by J. T. Bowen published by F. W. Greenough from McKenney and Hall. *Library of Congress, Prints & Photographs Division LC-USZC4-7311*

ABOVE: Jack Red Cloud, Oglala (Teton) Sioux, c. 1900, son of the famous Chief Red Cloud (left). The Red Clouds lived (and some descendants still do) on Pine Ridge. He wears an eagle feather trailer bonnet, a fine beaded shirt with shoulder and arm strips. He has a carved pipe stem and peace medal. He was photographed several times wearing this shirt: so, too, was his father indicating the attire belonged to the family. This was not always the case: photographers would often loan items of dress to enhance the image of their subjects if necessary. *Library of Congress, Prints & Photographs Division LC-USZ62-55849*

part in the Battle of Little Bighorn he escaped to Canada afterwards where descendants of his band remain. He surrendered at Ft. Burford in 1881 and spent his later years at Standing Rock. He became involved with the Ghost Dance movement and was killed by Indian police on December 15, 1890.

Standing Bear

Minneconjou (Teton) Sioux. Born on the Tongue River in 1859, he was a warrior at the Little Bighorn and led a successful war party against the Crows in 1879. He joined the Buffalo Bill Wild West Show traveling to Europe. He gave several interviews to historians giving personal details of the Custer battle. He died in 1934. As an exceptionally fine artist he has left some of the finest Indian art depicting the battle. Although a Minneconjou he lived among the Oglalas on the Pine Ridge Reservation

Standing Buffalo

Sisseton-Wahpeton (Santee) Sioux. He moved to Canada after the Minnesota uprising in 1862–63 and settled around Portage La Prairie and Ft. Garry, Manitoba. He later moved to a reserve in the Qu'Appelle Valley which still bears his name. His son White Cap obtained a separate reserve near Saskatoon.

Wanata (Charger)

Yanktonai Sioux. An important chief of the Pabaska (Cuthead) band of Yanktonai who was the son of Red Thunder and born about 1795, he served with his father on the British side during the War of 1812. His name "Charger" was given following his brave actions at the Battle of Ft. Sandusky where he was also wounded. After about 1820 he supported American interests and became heavily involved with the fur trade on the Missouri after removing from his

traditional home around Lake Traverse and the James River country. Later his influence waned and he was murdered by disaffected tribesmen c. 1848. Several other Wanata subsequently appeared and he has descendents at Spirit Lake, North Dakota.

Wabasha

Mdewakanton (Santee) Sioux. A dynasty of chiefs from the Kiyuksa villages in Minnesota bore this name. The "Great Wabasha" served with the British during the American Revolution and visited Mackinaw where he was welcomed by Col. De Peyster, British Commandant. Wabasha II came to prominence after meeting Lt. Zebulum Pike in 1806, but nominally supported the British in the War of 1812. He died c. 1855. Wabasha III signed the Laramie Treaty of 1868.

FAR LEFT: Kicking Bear (Mato Wanartaka) Oglala (Teton) Sioux—leader of a hostile band and priest of the Ghost Dance religion among the Sioux. Led the first dance on the Standing Rock Reservation in 1890 and was prominent in later hostilities for which he was held as a military prisoner. *The Art Archive/National Archives Washington D.C.*

CENTER LEFT: Sitting Bull, Hunkpapa (Teton) Sioux, spiritual leader. His childhood nickname was "Hunkeshnee" (thoughtful). The crucifix he is wearing was said to have been given to Sitting Bullby Fr. De Smet in 1868. Photograph by D. F. Barry, c. 1885. *Library of Congress, Prints & Photographs Division LC-USZ62-2315*

LEFT: Wabasha III, a principal Mdewakanton (Santee) Sioux chief at the time of the Minnesota War of 1862. He opposed the war.

LEFT: Monkaqushka, Trembling Earth, Yankton Sioux Chief. Signed a treaty in Washington in 1837, but died in Baltimore on October 25, 1837. A lithograph from a painting by George Cooke, from McKenney and Hall's The Indian Tribes of North America. *The Art Archive/ Bibliothèque des Arts Décoratifs Paris/Gianni Dagli Orti*

RIGHT: High Bear, Brulé (Teton) Sioux man wearing a long selvedged-edged trade cloth breechclout and holding a dance stick and dance shield. Rinehart photograph, Omaha, 1898.

FAR RIGHT: American Horse (Wasicu Tasunke) Oglala (Teton) Sioux. Possibly a nephew of the American Horse who signed the 1887 treaty that broke up the Great Sioux Reservation, he became a chief at Pine Ridge making several visits to Washington, including 1891 when he obtained fairer ration distribution for his people. He died in 1908. Photograph Rinehart, Omaha, 1898.

Bibliography

Bray, K. M.: *Making the Oglala Hoop: Oglala Sioux Political History, Pt.1: 1804–1825*; English Westerners Society, American Indian Studies Series No. 2, London, 1982.

Bray, K. M.: *Making the Oglala Hoop: Oglala Sioux Political History, Pt.II: 1825–1841* and *Pt.III 1841–1850*; English Westerners Society, American Indian Studies Nos. 4 & 5, London, 1985.

Brown, Joseph Epes: *The Sacred Pipe, Black Elk's Account of the Seven Rites of the Oglala Sioux*; Penguin Books Edition, 1972.

Carley, Kenneth: *The Sioux Uprising of 1862*; The Minnesota Historical Society, St. Paul, 1976.

Case, Ralph Hoyt: *One Hundred and First Anniversary of the Treaty of Ft Laramie 1851*; National Press Building, Washington DC, 1952.

Cowdrey, Mike and Martin, Ned and Jody: *American Indian Horse Masks*; Hawk Hill Press, Nicasio, California, 2006.

Ewers, J. E.: *Hairpipes in Plains Indian Adornment, a study in Indian and white ingenuity*; Anthropological Papers No. 50, Bureau of American Ethnology, Bull, 164, Washington DC, 1957.

Feder, Norman: *Art of the Eastern Plains Indians*; The Nathan Sturges Jarvis Collection, The Brooklyn, New York, 1964.

Green, Richard: *A Warrior I Have Been, Plains Indian Cultures in Transition*; Written Heritage, Louisiana, 2004.

Hail, Barbara A.: *Hau Kola, The Plains Indian Collection of the Haffenreffer Museum of Anthropology*; Brown University, Rhode Island, 1980.

Hardorff, Richard G.: *Lakota Recollections of the Custer Fight, New Sources of Indian Military History*; University of Nebraska Press, 1991.

Hook, Richard: *Warriors at the Little Bighorn 1876*; Osprey Publishing, Oxford, UK, 2004.

Howard, James H.: *The Canadian Sioux*; University of Nebraska Press, Lincoln and London, 1984.

Howard, James H.: *The Dakota or Sioux Tribe*; University of South Dakota, Museum News, Vermillion, South Dakota, 1966.

Johnson, Michael G.: *Encyclopedia of Native Tribes of North America (third edition)*; Compendium Publishing, London, UK, 2007.

Johnson, Michael G.: *Tribes of the Sioux Nation*; Osprey Publishing, Oxford, UK, 2000.

Meyer, Roy W.: *History of the Santee Sioux: United States Indian Policy on Trial*; University of Nebraska Press, Lincoln, 1993.

Norge, Ethel, Ed.: *The Modern Sioux, Social Systems and Reservation Culture*; University of Nebraska Press, Lincoln, 1970.

Powers, William K.: *Oglala Religion*; University of Nebraska Press, Lincoln, 1975.

Robinson, Doane: *A History of the Dakota or Sioux Indians*; Rossa Haines, Inc Reprint, Minneapolis, Minnesota, 1956.

Smith, J. L.: *A Short History of the Sacred Calf Pipe of the Teton Dakota*; Museum News, University of South Dakota, Vermillion, South Dakota, 1967.

Sturtevant, William C. (General Editor); DeMallie, Raymond J. (volume editor): *Handbook of North American Indians, Vol. 13, Pt.2: Plains*; Smithsonian Institution, Washington DC, 2001.

Tanner, Helen Hornbeck (ed): *Atlas of Great Lakes Indian History*; University of Oklahoma Press, Norman, 1987.

Taylor, Colin F.: *Analysis and Classification of the Plains Indians Ceremonial Shirt*; 5th Annual Plains Indian Seminar, Cody, Wyoming, 1981.

Various authors: *I Wear the Morning Star*; The Minneapolis Institute of Arts, Minneapolis, 1976.

Wallis, Wilson D.: *The Canadian Dakota*; Vol. 41: pt 1, Anthropological Papers of the American Museum of Natural History, New York, 1943.

White Bull, Joseph; translated and edited by Howard, James H.: *Lakota Warrior*; University of Nebraska Press, Bison Books edition, 1998.

Wissler, Clark: *Costumes of the Plains Indians*; Vol. 17 Anthropological Papers of the American Museum of Natural History, New York, 1915.

LEFT: Western Sioux and Arapaho delegation to Washington 1877. Standing Joe Merrivale; Young Spotted Tail; Antoine Janis (French-American fur trader); Seated: left to right, Touch-the-Clouds, Sioux; Sharp Nose, Black Coal, and Friday, all Arapahos. All the front chiefs are holding beaded pipe bags and pipes. *Library of Congress, Prints & Photographs Division LC-DIG-cwpbh-04312*